D1726921

Jumpstart to Digital Procurement

Wolfgang Schnellbächer · Daniel Weise

Jumpstart to Digital Procurement

Pushing the Value Envelope
in a New Age

 Springer

Wolfgang Schnellbächer
Boston Consulting Group
Stuttgart, Germany

Daniel Weise
Boston Consulting Group
Duesseldorf, Germany

ISBN 978-3-030-51983-4   ISBN 978-3-030-51984-1   (eBook)
https://doi.org/10.1007/978-3-030-51984-1

This Springer imprint is published by the registered company Springer Nature Switzerland AG.
The registered company address is: Gewerbestrasse 11, 6330 Cham, Switzerland

To Our Families

Acknowledgements

This book combines the knowledge of close to 100 Procurement projects with a digital focus in the last 2 years. It would not have been possible without the input of numerous colleagues through discussions on their work, access to their clients as interview partners or using the articles we jointly have published on their specific topics.

We are incredibly thankful to Alenka Triplat, Boris Sidopoulos, Christian Schuh, Dominik Steffani, Enes Oelcer, Florian Burgdorf, Georgina Lewis, Guillaume Gardy, Jens Esslinger, Martin Högel, Michael Jonas, Nina Haidinger, Nino Mori, Oliver Schubert, Raphael Desi, Rasmus Lund and Soren Biltoft-Knudsen.

Thank you

Contents

About the Authors

Wolfgang Schnellbächer is a Managing Director and Partner at Boston Consulting Group in Germany and leads procurement practice in Europe and the Middle East. Over the last 12 years, he has worked with companies like Daimler, Siemens, Thyssen-Krupp, RWE, BASF and Vattenfall on projects designed to help streamline existing procurement processes and incorporate new ideas and technologies. Here, Wolfgang's special focus has been on giving procurement a wider mandate to enable significantly increased savings but equally strong improvements in innovation, sustainability or quality. Wolfgang's doctoral thesis applied game theory to procurement negotiations and showed the difference between face-to-face and digital negotiation set-ups. The big passions in his personal life are literature and running.

Daniel Weise is a Managing Director and Partner of the Boston Consulting Group and the Global Lead of its procurement practice. In his 17 years with BCG, Daniel works exclusively in procurement consulting serving leading companies across industries and geographies. His work concentrates on unleashing the full value potential from procurement and implementing the best suiting operating models, also in special contexts like PMIs or turnaround cases. For him, digitization is at the core to enable the procurement team sustainably and to bolster companies' competitiveness—together with its supply base. In his free time, Daniel is a passionate mountaineer and a learning cook. Together with his family, he lives in Düsseldorf, Germany. Daniel holds a master's degree in business administration from WHU—Otto Beisheim School of Management and a master's degree in science of finance from London Business School.

List of Figures

A New Concept of Procurement

The revolution is coming and it will be big.

Digital disrupts our lives at an unparalleled pace. The interface between humans and machines has long been a source of anxiety, but this is now changing. Bots take over repetitive and mundane tasks. Artificial intelligence steers our decisions, from where to take our partnership to dinner to large investment choices. And blockchain builds trust, from diamond sourcing to day-to-day financial transactions.

This paradigm shift does not stop at the procurement function. However, we as procurement professionals struggle to find our narrative and, with that, a holistic concept to truly reap the benefits of the digital disruption. Few CPOs doubt that digital will strongly affect their function; however, only a handful claim that they are happy with the digital advancements they have made so far. Indeed, the majority of CPOs struggle to find a digital vision—a clear strategy to communicate with their employees, internal business partners, and suppliers. *Why do we have such a hard time explaining and benefitting from digital change in procurement?*

It is not that our expectations are too low. Savings ambitions of up to 20% are heralded, based on increased spend visibility and AI aiding negotiation preparation. Functions are supposed to become more efficient as a result of reducing the headcount by as much as 40%. Supplier relationships are to improve and employee motivation and skills are to increase. These expectations are shared by top management and even reflected in our companies' annual reports. Of the 20 largest Fortune 500 companies, 18 listed digital as a crucial topic in their annual reports, and 9 even stated that digital technologies are crucial for their procurement operations.

Furthermore, the tools and applications are neither scarce nor hard to access. Vendors in the market are really pushing them and CPOs everywhere would have an easy time filling up their calendars with new digital pitches from a wide variety of companies, ranging from large IT players to small start-ups.

The reason we as procurement professionals are lagging behind in our digital progress is much simpler: *we're involved in the wrong discussion.* When we talk digital, all we talk about is the individual tools. Whenever we meet, we discuss the pains and joys of Ariba, Coupa, and Synertrade, or the issues we have with our Blue

© Springer Nature Switzerland AG 2020
W. Schnellbächer, D. Weise, *Jumpstart to Digital Procurement*,
https://doi.org/10.1007/978-3-030-51984-1_1

Prism bots or another should-costing solution and, typically, we complain about the hurdles we face in their implementation. But we rarely take the discussion to a higher level, only occasionally ponder what we really need to create better value for our business. Sure enough, the more sophisticated among us plot the tools along the full source-to-pay process and find smart synergies, but we fail to clearly see what truly creates value in our particular situation. We need a new model, a revolutionary narrative of what procurement does on which to base our digital thinking. To put it more simply, if we want to make digital procurement with all its benefits real, we need to think differently.

The new thinking in procurement has to start with the value we create for our companies. In recent years, we have advanced from a function focusing purely on *savings* to a strategic partner that also secures access to critical *innovation* and the best *quality* from suppliers, ensures *sustainability* compliance throughout the supply chain and fast delivery *speed*, and limits the *risk* exposure in the supply market. Which of these six value dimensions is the most crucial varies from company to company, from procurement function to procurement function? Take, for example, the automotive industry where, in addition to savings, the OEMs focus on securing the right innovation for e-mobility or autonomous driving. Being the first mover here to secure exclusive access to critical suppliers is what leapfrogs companies, and this should be the focus of procurement's efforts.

It is different in the fashion retail industry where speed matters more, for example, getting the right clothing from Asian production sites into stores around the world before they go out of fashion. Another example is the consumer industry. Here, environmental and social standards across the supply chain are vital for avoiding accusations in the press of running sweatshops or of some other misdemeanor—so in this case, the crucial dimensions are likely to be savings, sustainability, and risk. Naturally, the value dimensions are also weighted differently within an industry, for example, there will be a difference between savings and quality depending on whether the company is striving to be a cost or a quality leader. Based on this overall direction, the right focus areas can then be selected and specific designs created at category level.

Each of these value dimensions is supported by enablers that make the procurement function work: the *organization*; the *process* landscape, that covers the definition of strategy setup processes all the way through to payment proceedings; the *people* working in the function with their skills and motivation; the *performance management* setup; and, lastly, the *collaboration* with internal business partners and suppliers. CPOs need to choose which of these enablers best support their particular value dimensions. Take our automotive OEM again—for innovation purposes it should invest in securing collaboration and smart performance management to incentivize suppliers to produce good ideas. The retailer with the need for speed should take care to ensure a smart and agile process setup, while the producer of consumer goods needs to have people dedicated to risk management and rigid sustainability auditing processes. Once clear on the weighting of the value dimensions, the enablers need to be designed accordingly.

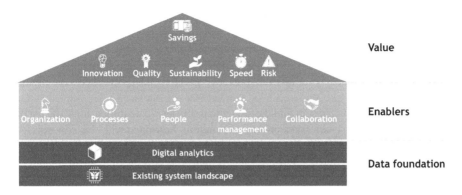

Fig. 1 BCG's Procurement House

All procurement decisions should be founded on data and analytics, be it on the value or the enabler dimension. The digital analytics themselves need to be connected to the existing systems and databases and this is what lays the foundation for our Procurement House (see Fig. 1).

This Procurement House forms the basis for our digital discussions. Based on the primary value we generate for our business, based on transparency in terms of the enablers that best support this value, we can choose the right tools and applications. If we want to concentrate on *savings*, we can chose between tail spend management solutions, automated bidding, or dynamic should-costing models, depending on which spend buckets seem to pack the most potential. A powerful example is AI negotiation coach that learns over time, advising buyers of which negotiation approach to use in what situations, from traditional face-to-face setups to complex multistage auctions, from linear performance pricing (LPP) to collaborative cost-out conventions.

If it is primarily a question of *quality*, live reporting tools may be the method of choice. These apps are installed on the mobile devices of users on site and the users report in real time how they perceive the quality of delivery. The feedback is displayed on comprehensive dashboards visible to procurement, business partners, and suppliers alike. If *speed* is crucial to the business, the procurement team should be investing in robots that ensure fast transactions or chatbots that explain to users how to best fill purchase requisitions that can be quickly transformed into purchase orders. In terms of *innovation* for collaboration platforms with suppliers and to prevent *risk* or *sustainability* issues, buyers should leverage AI algorithms that tell buyers up front where the next incident is likely to happen, empowered by visibility into the whole supply chain.

Tools and applications can be linked to each of the enabler dimensions. For illustration purposes, let us take a look at two dimensions. In developing our digital capability in *people*, assessments can build tailored curriculums for each buyer and track their learning progress against these goals. In *performance management*, digital tools can much more easily extract the requisite data from various systems and add it to tailored dashboards containing the right KPIs for each role. Equally, each of the enabler dimensions needs to be set up in a manner that best supports the digital revolution. New roles, such as robotic maintenance engineers or AI programmers, need to be introduced to the *organization*, *processes* need to be more clearly described and, if necessary, adapted so they can be automated. *Collaboration* with suppliers and internal business partners needs to focus on digital innovation.

Based on this new concept and the strategic priorities/value dimensions, the list of digital tools and use cases takes on a clear structure. Equipped with this concept, we can now take a closer look at procurement's digital future. The following chapters provide a deep-dive into each of the value dimensions and they are all structured in the same way: Following a brief introduction, we discuss the starting position by introducing conventional best practices for acing in that value dimension and the resulting challenges that remain to be tackled. Next, we explain how digital can help resolve those challenges and we describe which enablers are required to facilitate implementation of the digital solutions. Last, we provide an outlook on the topics that will most likely become relevant for procurement managers in the near future.

Part I

Value: Whatever Matters to the Business

Savings: The Right Applications for the Right Spend

Let us start at the top of the house. Without a doubt, savings is the most important value dimension for the majority of CPOs. Consequently, it is methods of generating savings that are the most developed among the six value dimensions. Best-in-class companies combine a rigid strategic sourcing approach based on comprehensive category strategies with the right tactical selection of enablers tailored to the specific sourcing situation. For example, successful savings generation may require strong collaboration with business partners to prevent costly over-specifications and unnecessary demand while ensuring that specifications do not limit the supplier landscape.

Savings strategies are typically tailored to sourcing categories and they build on a set of commercial and technical levers that are each assessed in terms of their applicability to the situation at hand. For commercial levers, for example, savings are generated by reviewing the supply base in order to reduce the total number of suppliers. The implementation of such levers is then facilitated by purchasing systems and tools. A spend cube enables segmentation of data by category, location, and suppliers and helps to identify which levers can be best used within and across different categories. For technical levers, for example, best-in-class companies use catalysts to create savings. A typical method involves workshops—suppliers are invited to a 1-day event to identify cost-reduction opportunities with the buyer.

However, even companies that lead in terms of the strategic sourcing process are nowhere near to fully exploiting the savings potential. In fact, there are three digital levers that will become critical to successful savings generation going forward.

1. Real-time analytics: Getting your data together
2. AI-based buyer steering: Machines thinking smarter than us
3. Automated tail spend management: Tackling the untackleable

© Springer Nature Switzerland AG 2020
W. Schnellbächer, D. Weise, *Jumpstart to Digital Procurement*,
https://doi.org/10.1007/978-3-030-51984-1_2

Real-Time Analytics: Getting Your Data Together

Identifying the true savings potential in a given category or purchasing situation can prove quite difficult. We asked 15 CPOs across industries how satisfied they were with the ways in which their category managers identify such opportunities. On a scale ranging from "completely satisfied" to "completely lack transparency in this field," only two indicated utmost satisfaction. Another five said they were "somewhat satisfied" and eight even admitted to a complete lack of such transparency.

A closer look at the survey results reveals two main imperatives for CPOs: First, they must adopt a fact-based internal perspective to determine realistic savings targets for their category managers and, second, they must create a fact-based external perspective to guide managers toward selecting the right negotiation approaches. The answer to these challenges has been the same for many years: price transparency tools, such as should-cost models or linear performance pricing (LPP) tools, can generate valuable insights. However, despite their extensive benefits, the usage of such tools has been limited. Fortunately, the digital revolution is completely changing the game.

Starting Position: A Big Toolbox but Little Data

When contemplating the ways CPOs guide their category managers toward creating savings and preparing for negotiations, some unfortunate facts become obvious. Category managers often do not know what exactly they are buying and to which supplier they should ideally award the business. They lack demand forecasts, which would indicate how their spend volumes will develop in the future and allow suppliers to make the right investment or disinvestment choices, despite the fact that the company actually possesses the volume information—it simply has not been conveyed to the procurement function. In addition, category managers lack transparency regarding the different cost buckets for each product and the options available for making those products cheaper. When it comes to using price transparency tools, they often lack the required data or, worse still, they do not know what tools they should use or how they should interpret and leverage the results once the tools have been applied.

When considering the latter issue, in particular, price transparency tools can support category managers in their decision-making. They range from component teardowns to the analysis of contract setups and they focus on price plausibility, awarding analytics, and even idea generation. Overall, they can be structured into three layers: comparing single cost buckets (e.g., labor costs), comparing parts or SKUs, or comparing suppliers (see Fig. 1).

To *compare cost buckets*, category managers primarily use price transparency tools to create price plausibility (e.g., raw material benchmarking or commercial should-cost modeling) and ideation around design improvement (e.g., target costing or teardowns). Commercial should-cost models have proven an impactful method, especially for developing price plausibility. They monitor the cost of all the buckets

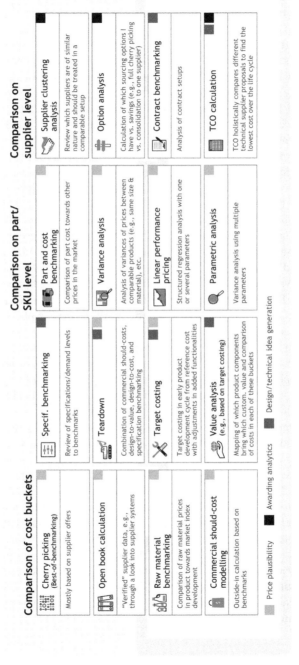

Comparison of cost buckets

Cherry picking (Best-of-benchmarking)

Mostly based on supplier offers

Open book calculation

"Verified" supplier data, e.g., through a look into supplier systems

Raw material benchmarking

Comparison of raw material prices in product towards market index development

Commercial should-cost modelling

Outside-in calculation based on benchmarks

Specif. benchmarking

Review of specifications/demand levels to benchmarks

Teardown

Combination of commercial should-costs, design-to-value, design-to-cost, and specification benchmarking

Target costing

Target costing in early product development cycle from reference cost with adjustments in added functionalities

Value analysis (e.g., based on target costing)

Mapping of which product components bring which custom. value and comparison of costs in each of these buckets

Comparison on part/ SKU level

Part and cost benchmarking

Comparison of part cost towards other prices in the market

Variance analysis

Analysis of variances of prices between comparable products (e.g., same size & material), etc.

Linear performance pricing

Structured regression analysis with one or several parameters

Parametric analysis

Variance analysis using multiple parameters

Comparison on supplier level

Supplier clustering analysis

Review which suppliers are of similar nature and should be treated in a comparable setup

Option analysis

Calculation of which sourcing options I have vs. savings (e.g., full cherry picking vs. consolidation to one supplier)

Contract benchmarking

Analysis of contract setups

TCO calculation

TCO holistically compares different technical supplier proposals to find the lowest cost over the life cycle

Price plausibility   Awarding analytics   Design/technical idea generation

Fig. 1 Price transparency toolbox

of the supplier's product and compare the total cost with the price the supplier is asking for. The result is a comparison of the actual and should cost, showing clear improvement potential. For example, an aerospace and technology innovation leader used a should-cost model to challenge the costs of one of its civil application radar systems. The cross-functional team, consisting of a category manager, several engineers (mechanical, electrical, radio frequency), and a procurement cost engineer, identified savings potential of 25%. On confronting the supplier with the results, the supplier agreed to a rigorous design-to-value/design-to-cost exercise. Changes in technology (i.e., different encoding technology), process (i.e., simplifying documentation and testing requirements), and logistics (i.e., switching from shipping the surveillance antenna as a whole to shipping it in parts) brought costs down as requested and ultimately led to price reductions of 18%.

On a *part or SKU level*, transparency tools are used for plausibility purposes to review price levels (e.g., part and cost benchmarking, variance analysis, linear performance pricing (LPP)). LPP is a prime example. When a component has a parameter that is a main cost driver, it can be plotted on a scatter chart. Outliers become obvious and help quantify the cost-savings potential. A Nordic dairy company used LPP to identify price reduction opportunities after having decided to integrate all international markets into its global procurement structure. Corrugated boxes represented a large spend bucket and the responsible category manager was curious as to how plausible the pricing of the boxes was in each of the countries. Therefore, the weight of the box along with some other specification data was collected and outliers were found for two of the five suppliers in North America. Having this information helped achieve savings of up to 20% on the outlier boxes.

Last, on a *supplier level*, category managers use price transparency tools predominantly for awarding scenarios/analytics, like option analysis, and for ideation for design improvement ideas, such as calculating the total cost of ownership (TCO). The latter can help in determining the impact of all cost buckets on the TCO. It provides insights into an optimal product configuration, for example. When a Swedish chemicals producer was faced with leasing several new trucks, the responsible category manager mapped all the cost components, such as the initial investment costs and the fixed and variable operating costs, to form an understanding of the optimal vehicle configuration. The result helped determine which engine type they should choose, the recommended maximum mileage, and the optimal contract duration, to name but a few specifications. Demand forecast tools can be applied equally well at supplier level. They collect sales information and forecasts directly from the sales force of the buying company and translate it directly into supplier-specific forecasts detailing exactly the parts each supplier produces. A global machinery company faced massive supplier complaints because any information given to suppliers was either late or oftentimes not corrected. This meant—and the supply base was very open about this—that additional costs were being charged to the machining producer.

Remaining Challenges

In the past, transparency tools were both generally known and selectively applied, however, they were never used as extensively as they could have been to enhance value generation. Digital is now changing that in three ways:

- Ensuring sufficient data is available to conduct comprehensive analyses.
- Reducing the workload for buyers in analytics setups.
- Real-time supplier follow-ups.

How Digital Is Changing the Game: Real-Time Analytics Solutions

Ensuring Sufficient Data Is Available to Conduct Comprehensive Analyses

Each analysis tool depends on the availability of the right data sets, and digitization will heavily support this core requirement going forward. For example, data is not usually stored centrally but is often found to be highly decentralized (e.g., in BU-specific systems or storage folders with multiple scanned invoices in PDF form). Going forward, big data will combine fragmented data sources into comprehensive overviews that lay the foundation for further analyses. Here, big data will leverage the knowledge stored in systems in which a large amount of especially commercial information can be found. This is particularly true in accounting systems that pay invoices electronically. With technical data, the situation is slightly different. While some information is stored in various engineering systems (e.g., CAD), plenty of technical data cannot be found in a dedicated system at all. To gather such dispersed information, data crawlers will come into play. They feed big data overviews by scrolling through large data dumps in files in all kinds of formats using a defined heuristic logic. For example, every time the word *material* or *material number* appears, the data crawler will assume that the stored information describes a material. The output is then matched with other material descriptions and cross-checked with predefined exclusion rules. An exclusion rule might mean that when the detected material description contains a unit of measurement such as kilogram, the data crawler will assume that the information is not likely to describe a material type.

The increased availability of data also opens up an entirely new cosmos of analytics opportunities. Contract management platforms are able to analyze all core contract parameters (e.g., payment terms) and thus enable large-scale payment term optimization initiatives with suppliers. The same opportunities also exist for price plausibility analyses. In the past, category managers had to decide up front what variance analysis they would conduct. Afterward, data had to be collected in the hope that the initial assumption was correct and that the analysis ultimately revealed savings potential. Now, based on an enhanced data set, numerous price transparency tools are used in parallel and in real time. The results enable category managers to immediately track product price variances over time and compare different BUs and products with similar technical specifications. A German utility company, for example, installed data crawlers and leveraged available data to prepare for a supplier day. The event was hosted with the intention of saving €200 million. The crawlers collected large amounts of data that were then used to create price transparency at product/SKU level. The company conducted LPP, price variance analyses over time and for different locations, and even online searches for alternative prices for existing products. This new level of transparency was then leveraged during the supplier day by directly asking potential suppliers for alternative quotes for selected parts. Overall, the supplier day helped create savings of 18% on those parts, while 90% stayed with incumbent suppliers. The power of analytics was great enough to break the resistance of incumbent suppliers to grant price concessions.

At a cost bucket level, digital also enables more powerful analytics, such as big data repositories or automated data collection. Should-cost models, for example, can be made dynamic and fed with the most recent information on different cost buckets (see also the section below).

Reducing the Workload for Buyers in Analytics Setups

Digital will support a large number of analysis activities that category managers used to perform manually. Based on the big data overviews described, robots are set up to conduct comprehensive analyses on a repetitive basis. For example, while category managers usually perform LPP by hand, digital tools now run this automatically—based on predefined schedules. Monthly variance analyses and even multivariate LPP can help to highlight price outliers in real time and thus facilitate the development of negotiation plans. They provide full transparency on cost differences across suppliers and the category manager is automatically informed of outliers at SKU level and can follow this up with suppliers.

> **How It Has Been Done: Automated Price Calculations at an Automotive Tier 1 Supplier**
>
> *When comparing cost buckets, the positive effects of robotics come into play, in the form of dynamic should-cost models. An American automotive tier 1 supplier, for example, decided to set up dynamic should-cost models with its core suppliers in standard categories (e.g., stamping, fasteners, fineblanking). The models defined the component cost for each SKU, split into raw materials, energy, labor, logistics, overheads, and margin. Each month, the price development of these components was tracked dynamically and, with that tracking, the respective supplier cost of each SKU. Category managers could then focus their efforts on those suppliers in order to negotiate price reductions. And, in times of declining prices, buyers could even leverage the available data to back large tenders and host supplier days. In the long term, more and more should-cost models served as hardwired tools to*

(continued)

derive target prices that also defined the cost of future parts, based on cost-input parameters, taking commercial risks from the supplier side into consideration. In addition to the technical analysis, strong focus was placed on sufficient supplier incentives for aligning technical improvements up front, such as increased speed in coil change time or improved efficiency in press handling. In addition to price transparency, it had to be ensured that suppliers still placed sufficient emphasis on innovation in these highly cost relevant fields. Strict quotas were set which, for example, improved the coil change time at large presses from 60 to 30 min.

For more complex parts and submodules, product teardowns are typically used to identify cost-reduction opportunities and ideate design improvements. Digital technology in the form of augmented reality robotics and wearables will significantly decrease both cost and lead time and increase the ease of usage for such teardowns.

How It Has Been Done: Using Digital Solutions to Identify Savings via Design Change Scenarios
Recently, a cross-functional team of procurement and engineering employees was looking for breakthrough savings in a complex subassembly consisting of optical, electronic, and mechanical parts. They decided to purchase a competitor product that supposedly had a 15% cost advantage. However, the cost of the product was €500,000, which would have been lost as the product could not be resold after having been taken apart. However, with relatively simple scanning technology and an augmented reality application, the team was able to decompose the product without loosening a screw. With the help of wearables, they were able to identify the individual components and a software program helped calculate the basic parameters such as weight and density. In parallel, a robot application checked the used parts in the competitor product against the data and drawings available in the CAD system to quickly identify apparent differences. Within minutes, a report was created that highlighted the main differences. Given the link to the CAD system or engineering software, the engineers could easily test initial hypotheses (e.g., using thinner or different materials or using different technologies such as optical versus mechanical encoding). Based on this first assessment, a long list of viable design change scenarios was created and prioritized for execution.

Real-Time Supplier Follow-Ups
As spend analytics become automated, the opportunity arises to also follow up with suppliers in real time. Robots communicate outliers to suppliers and internal business partners. In the case of business partners, the digital tools collect information to

verify initial assumptions, such as whether the given data on price outliers is correct. If all the requisite information is verified, robots can assist in setting up supplier communication and even start negotiation.

Taking the example of the payment terms mentioned as an outcome of contract analysis, robots can take the information about all the suppliers who have old payment terms and inform them via automatically generated e-mails about the new payment terms to be applied going forward. Without the category manager needing to be involved, large amounts of information can be selected and scanned, and respective conclusions can be drawn. Even the required supplier follow-ups can be taken care of in real time: Robots can pre-formulate answers to supplier responses, clustered on the basis of keywords contained in supplier responses. A large automotive OEM did this for its indirect spend and digitized and analyzed 5000 contracts within 6 weeks. The analysis revealed that ~2000 had unfavorable payment terms and, as a result, respective suppliers were approached and asked to adjust those terms. Here, five reactions to supplier responses were pre-formulated. They ranged from a brief "Thank you" if the supplier's response contained keywords of acceptance to a threat if the supplier's response was harsh and indicative of escalation. No answer was sent without the category manager's approval, but all agreed that even if they had to modify the responses, it was possible to conduct the entire operation much faster than with conventional methods. It took only another 5 weeks to put standard payment terms into place for 80% of these contracts.

How It Has Been Done: Bid Optimization at a Telecommunications Company

In early rounds of RfP processes (when many suppliers are still in the race for possible contract awards), a global telecommunications company used robots to give suppliers price feedback at cost bucket level. Leveraging cherry-picking (best-of benchmarking), the robots were programmed to provide real-time feedback on a supplier's quote. Specifically, they gave feedback on the completeness of the quote, highlighted implausible outliers based on a predefined threshold, and set price reduction ranges to be adhered to if the supplier wanted to be considered in the next round. Furthermore, the robot gave an indication of which cost bucket suppliers should focus on based on a simple comparison of other suppliers' responses to the requested cost breakdown. That way, the buyer automated the follow-up of incomplete quotes and the tedious process of first-round price feedback. Not only were the results of the RfP improved through the process, the buyers were also relieved of a lot of manual and redundant effort.

Looking Ahead

Analytics should form the backbone of every procurement initiative. In the past, procurement professionals were equipped with a powerful toolkit for their activities—especially for savings generation. However, seldom were they able to apply the tools with the right scale and speed. A lack of data, resources, and at times even capabilities prevented them from doing so. Now, in the digital age, all these hurdles can be overcome and analytics can take its rightful place at the center of the preparations for any supplier or business partner discussion focusing on cost improvements.

AI-Based Buyer Steering: Machines Thinking Smarter Than Us

Once companies have the right data sets available and real-time calculation mechanisms in place, the next challenge that arises is choosing the most fitting tool for each purchasing situation. This is true for commercial and technical optimization approaches, where all the analytical tools we just saw play a key role, but equally for interactive mechanisms, such as cost-out conventions or supplier workshops. Finally, choosing the right tool is crucial in go-to-market approaches for confronting suppliers. Here too, a wide range of tools is available: for example, English, Dutch, or Japanese auction setups, supplier days, parallel negotiations, or expressive bidding mechanisms in which different specification options form part of the bidding process.

Starting Position: The Big Question of Which Tool to Use

In theory, it is quite clear which tool to use when. LPP is most powerful within fragmented spend, for example. English auctions are a stronger go-to-market approach compared with conventional negotiations in a highly competitive market characterized by strong rivalry. However, in reality, procurement organizations consistently underutilize or misapply the full procurement toolkit. Negotiations are still most commonly conducted face-to-face with few or no supporting tools used, leaving large savings on the table. Auctions in particular, though popularized more than two decades ago, are only employed to a small extent and often only in the more traditional English auction style despite the broad spectrum of powerful options.

In an analysis of 15 procurement functions across industries, we compared the actual go-to-market approach and supporting commercial and technical optimization tools used to those recommended for the specific situation. The results were clear: Procurement teams are not consistently applying best practices when they select negotiation approaches and supporting tools. In fact, only 15% of the cases were the most powerful tool chosen (see Fig. 2).

But why are not buyers using the right tools even if all the supporting data is available? It is not a lack of understanding, as there is a best-in-class toolbox with

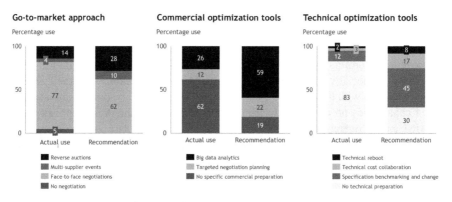

Fig. 2 Go-to-market approaches and commercial and technical optimization tools used versus the AI negotiation coach's best practice recommendations

detailed descriptions available in almost every function. Instead, our experience suggests that the challenge lies in convincing even the most experienced and capable buyers to think beyond the traditional. To make things more complex, more "advanced" approaches and tools are not necessarily better—the core consideration must be whether the approach is suited to the category and context. In our study, we found multiple cases in which advanced tools were used in the wrong scenarios and, unsurprisingly, had limited success. For example, in one case an English auction was conducted in a relationship-focused oligopoly where a traditional face-to-face negotiation would have been more powerful. The auction, though advanced and digitally enabled, was not suited to the low-competition scenario so it lacked the aggressive bidding typical of an English auction, making it too obvious to the supplier that they were in a powerful position with low competitive threat. In the past, CPOs and consultants have also contributed to this misapplication of advanced approaches and tools, sometimes instituting quotas for the use of more advanced approaches and supporting tools, such as a target for the number of auctions conducted in a given year. This is equally as wrong as exclusively using "simple" approaches and tools, as an approach or tool will not deliver a better result simply because it is more complex or "advanced" than others.

Remaining Challenge

Even if all the data is available to fill the right analytical tools, all the resources on hand to drive technical optimization workshops, and there is a strong competitive situation for powerful go-to-market approaches, buyers very often make the wrong choices on which purchasing tools to apply.

How Digital Is Changing the Game: AI-Steered Negotiations

AI negotiation coaches tackle this challenge by leveraging game theory logic to recommend a go-to-market approach and supporting optimization tools that are best suited to each scenario—and therefore most likely to deliver the best outcomes. Based on the collective procurement team feedback and savings outcomes, the coaches apply machine-learning algorithms to refine their recommendations to identify the optimum combination of go-to-market approaches and commercial and technical optimization tools for each scenario, thereby connecting the brains of the entire function.

When applying an AI negotiation coach, it is crucial to balance outside-in knowledge of best-in-class procurement with the category expertise within the procurement team. Advanced tools form the core of the base digital toolkit, but the toolkit also includes simpler tools such as benchmarking and raw material index analysis. In total, the current standard version of BCG's coach recommends over 10,000 combinations of 100 approaches and tools, following a typical set of 10–15 questions. The base logic is then adapted to reflect the organization's procurement setup, such as category names and savings database links. For advanced organizations, AI negotiation coaches can be more broadly adapted to include additional go-to-market approaches and the supporting tools desired, plus the opportunity to tailor the game theory logic and machine learning. This is typically done in one or two collaborative workshops with the procurement team in order to create a strong logic that combines outside-in best practice with the existing buyer expertise and toolkit. For example, if should-cost modeling is a strong capability, it could be further differentiated to define use cases for multiple variants, such as parametric pricing models. Strongly involving lead buyers in these workshops brings not only their expertise but also the additional advantage of increasing buy-in for the future tool rollout. Figure 3 shows one such workshop with the logic tree developing in the background. This logic tree must capture all the information to be taught to the AI negotiation coach in each case.

The logic tree must be clear and unambiguous, demand objective responses, and, most importantly, each question must be a step by which the recommendation will be defined. For example, one prerequisite for a powerful LPP analysis use case is having fragmented spend; the associated question would be, "Is the spend fragmented?" Similarly, to perform an auction, at least three or more suppliers should be available; the associated question would therefore be, "How many suppliers do you believe will participate and submit a bid?" If the scenario fulfills this requirement, the following questions should then apply further rules and prerequisites to refine the design of the auction, whether it is English, Dutch, or Japanese, and where it should be on the spectrum ranging from fully transparent to completely concealed.

For more advanced organizations, the AI coach can be integrated into existing systems to extract responses to questions, thereby preventing duplication of buyer input and ensuring the accuracy of responses. Questions that can be answered automatically might include the category, the number of bidders, and the volume

Fig. 3 Workshop defining the AI negotiation coach logic

of SKUs in order to establish the fragmentation of spend. This is, of course, optional and the AI negotiation coach can be rolled out both as an integrated tool within an existing digital procurement toolkit or as a standalone tool.

After the initial rollout, the AI negotiation coach can provide a go-to-market approach and supporting tool recommendations to the buyers using the tailored logic tree. During the rollout, it is important to communicate to the buyers that the AI negotiation coach recommendation is not binding. It should be considered in combination with the buyer's category expertise. However, buyers who consistently override the AI negotiation coach recommendation to favor traditional approaches and tools should be challenged by procurement leadership to step outside their comfort zone. In larger awarding processes, this should be challenged in sourcing committees, while managers can leverage the aggregate reporting from the AI negotiation coach to see patterns in smaller awarding processes.

As buyers use the coach and record the success of the savings of each combination of approaches and tools for each category, the machine-learning algorithms learn which combinations are most powerful to deliver the optimum result. Similar to connecting the logic tree to existing digital systems, if savings tracking already exists in another system such as SAP Ariba or Synertrade, this data can be regularly imported into the AI negotiation coach. The machine-learning algorithms adapt the recommendations based on which outcomes were recommended, which were selected, and what final savings resulted. For example, if the buyers of a certain category select a Dutch auction, despite the coach recommendation of an English auction, and are consistently more successful with this approach, the coach will learn from these results that a Dutch auction is more powerful in this category and modify the recommendation going forward—not just for that buyer but for all those sourcing within that category and context. Thus the coach learns over time and combines the brains of all the buyers in a function by combining all of their experience into a large "intuition machine." This dynamic adaptation of behavior also guarantees that suppliers are never able to use their experience to draw any conclusions about the amount or type of competition on the basis of the negotiation approach used, since the use of the different approaches and tools remains dynamic. The procurement team can revisit the logic tree and recommendations in order to include new options as the procurement toolkit matures, while trying to identify new logic patterns. One example entered additionally into the coach was, "What is the age of the selling counterpart?" This question was then included in the standard question set to try to detect patterns for its recommendations based on buyer input. In the case of age however, unsurprisingly, no patterns have yet been identified that affect the recommendations.

How It Has Been Done: The Coach in Real Life—6% Savings in 12 Months

We introduced BCG's AI Negotiation Coach at a large automotive tier 1 supplier, known in the market for its aggressive buying behavior and skillful buyers. The starting point was a target increase of 3% on direct and 5% on indirect spend coming from the CPO asking for a procurement contribution in tense times. This request came at a time when the function had seen several years of record savings that had led to a feeling of exhaustion among buyers and strong pushback from the supplier side. Furthermore, the majority of award processes were tenders, despite the buyers having access to a broad and advanced procurement toolkit. The CPO therefore introduced the coach not only to regain momentum and restore an element of fun with game-theory-based thinking, but also to steer his buyers away from the almost exclusive use of traditional techniques. The procurement function was quite mature, so it was deeply involved in both the development of the initial coach logic and in developing an associated capability building program to relaunch the full procurement toolkit. One manager was so closely engaged, he even went so far as to hang the original decision tree in his office as a large poster. In addition to this deep involvement, the CPO demanded full acceptance of the recommendations given by the AI Negotiation Coach, or compelling logic for deviating from them, as well as consistent updates to the coach on savings achieved and approaches and tools used. The results backed him up. While the 3% savings target in direct spending was met in spite of all the doubts of the function's experts, the indirect team even overshot the 5% target, achieving 7% in savings. Especially in medium spend buckets where there was a significant increase in the use of many types of auctions, the success was far above expectations. Moreover, the teams found that the coach helped them to complete tenders faster, enabling them to meet savings targets even with multiple vacancies across the function. In addition to the impressive savings, the coach supported a shift in behavior, resulting in a clear improvement in

(continued)

the mood within the function and a renewed positive reaction to analytical approaches. Across the teams, new approaches to negotiations and analytical tools were discussed much more frequently and buyers admitted that these conversations and problem-solving efforts made their job more fun!

Looking Ahead

Behavioral steering for negotiation preparation and execution is one of the leading applications of AI in procurement. While AI rollouts are oftentimes slowed down due to a lack of sufficient data, here the initial hypotheses can be built on game theory and similar heuristics, and AI can learn on that basis. Combined with the high value they are able to provide in generating savings, AI negotiation coaches will remain one of the core applications in the digital journeys of procurement functions.

Automated Tail Spend Management: Tackling the Untackleable

Managing tail spend is a difficult task for procurement teams. But thanks to digital tools, this is changing rapidly. Digital tools provide insight into the millions of purchases made every year, helping companies understand and manage their tail spend at an unprecedented level of detail. And with the maturation of big data and advanced analytics, AI, automation, and digital platforms, companies can even completely eliminate some of their tail spend; firms that use digital tools to manage tail spend can cut their annual expenditures by as much as 5–10%.

Starting Position: Managing a Large Number of Items

Tail spend is defined as the amount of money that an organization spends on purchases that make up approximately 80% of transactions but only 20% of total spend volume. Yet what constitutes tail spend varies by category; for example, machine parts for industrial goods companies, specialty chemical materials for chemicals companies, and office supplies for banks. The number of tail spend items also varies: a turbine manufacturer may have more than 130,000 items, while a bank will probably have far less.

Most procurement functions devote but little attention to their tail spend, mostly because of the complexity involved. It affects a large number of transactions, many categories, and a huge and largely anonymous supplier base. A large chemicals company, for example, can have more than 3000 suppliers—and that is just for direct materials. As such, the complexity involved requires a lot of resources, something that most procurement functions do not have. It is easier to simply let the ordering plants handle orders, negotiations, and the overall supplier management with all of its inherent complexity.

Moreover, tail items are not usually a top priority. They are purchased only once every 2 or 3 years, so they are often overlooked in discussions with suppliers. Procurement managers tend to focus instead on more strategic spend: 20% of suppliers that account for 80% of total spend volume.

Firms that have been able to devote resources to tail spend management use only a few tactics. First, they use *standardization and bundling* to harmonize the specifications of components used in different products in order to reduce the total number of tail items. Consolidating suppliers in groups make collaboration easier. Second, they put as many tail spend articles as possible into *catalogs* to make standardization and bundling sustainable. AI can then analyze the spend data to provide guidance on which items should be procured this way. Catalogs are popular because they offer only one option and one supplier for each item. However, they can be difficult to work with and, since they are updated infrequently, they do not always provide the parts or services needed. Catalogs are also good for corporate governance because they enforce spending regulations. They proactively support compliance by offering only a small number of items rather than a whole assortment. This reduces the number of SKUs significantly and, more importantly, it can reduce transactional cost by as much as 30–40% per transaction. Third, firms use *purchasing cards* to automatically record who is buying what and how often, while ensuring that the order process runs smoothly. Overall, this process is highly efficient and the prices of components and services are lower than where other methods are used. Last, firms use *outsourcing* to third parties to handle tail spend: a company that focuses entirely on tail spend is probably able to optimize savings and has better economies of scale than others. However, outsourcing also means depending on a single provider, which can hamper flexibility and innovation.

Remaining Challenges

Standardization, bundling, catalogs, purchasing cards, and outsourcing to third parties can help prevent tail spend from growing further. However, procurement functions are still grappling with the more basic challenges.

- They do not have sufficient transparency for commercial and technical purchases.
- The huge volumes of manual work make it difficult to manage tail spend effectively.

Fortunately, digital technologies can address these challenges in the future.

How Digital Is Changing the Game: Bringing Transparency to the Blind Spots

Creating Tail Spend Transparency

The key to managing tail spend is to analyze the underlying data. In the past, most spend data was largely inaccessible. Today, digital technologies allow companies to develop an overview of the spend baseline by automatically collecting and assessing different types of data: (1) internal spend data, (2) supplementing PO data, and (3) supplier data.

Internal spend data (that is, e.g., data from purchase orders (POs) or invoices) used to be hard to collect, being generally stored in PDFs in different systems across the company. Now, thanks to consolidation programs, it is possible to combine data from various systems into one view. Data-crawling robots can go through fragmented files and collect information by looking for a unique part number or description. And a software solution can then scan the lists of items and suppliers to see if any are recorded under multiple names. For example, a supplier could be listed as BASF Germany, BASF AG, or Badische Anilin & Sodafabrik—all of which refer to the same company. Afterward, procurement managers can conduct a spend cube analysis for expenditures across categories, business units, and suppliers. This data can also shed light on the tail spend per sub-category; the extent of fragmentation in the supplier base; the range of prices for any given item across suppliers, sites, volume, and time; and the proportion of spend managed by the procurement function, devoted to catalogs, and so on.

Supplementing spend data can help whenever spend data is insufficient. Drawing and non-drawing-based information excellence tools, for example, can help companies determine whether various machine parts are identical or merely similar. Advanced analytics can also help by detecting when slight differences in the product specifications of different tail items lead to unnecessarily high handling costs. When a manufacturing company, for example, needed to gain better insight into approximately $400 million of annual miscellaneous spend, it used an algorithm to analyze technical data sheets, drawings, and specifications. The algorithm found thousands of duplications and similar parts that could be harmonized by one click, eliminating those redundancies cut down expense entries by 30%.

Once data is collected from various sources, an AI algorithm can scan it for errors and fix them. If the algorithm notices, for example, that the weight of a spare part is entered as 1000 kg, it can look to see whether 1000 g might be more plausible. Algorithms can also mine invoices and other documents to provide information missing from PO data.

Last, *supplier data* can be brought in by simply asking suppliers for missing information. Here digital collection platforms are helpful. Instead of requiring suppliers to fill an empty page with all kinds of unnecessary information, the platform provides a partially completed form with just a few blanks for the supplier to fill in. This makes the process easier for suppliers—and makes it more likely that they will complete the form. Companies can also extract pricing information from external benchmarks to create a database across parts, suppliers, business units, countries, and so on. AI tools can then compare prices and alert buyers when favorable buying conditions arise.

Managing Tail Spend More Efficiently

Once procurement functions have a good sense of what their tail spend looks like, they can use a variety of digital tools to manage it more efficiently. For example, they can use *mass tenders*, which used to be extremely challenging due to the large number of items and suppliers involved. In the past, requests for information required a great deal of effort from a buying company, mostly because of the high annual volume of requests and the lack of accessible data especially on less critical parts and services. Today *eRfIs* can be issued to many suppliers and distributors around the world with an automated read-out of all filled-in data points. The vendors, in turn, provide information about the products they can supply. The number of distributors in each country for each product can then be illustrated in a heat map (see Fig. 4).

The information generated by the *eRfI* and the heat map serve as the basis for an *eRfQ*. In a mass tender, a supplier would have to wade through thousands of line items in a list rather than the few hundred it could actually provide. Many vendors would not want to take the time to identify those items because of the low profit involved. Often, suppliers would only provide quotes for some of the items they could supply rather than for all of them, which made the tail even longer. *eRfQ* platforms dispense with this problem because they allow each distributor to see only the line items that that company can provide. After the distributors have submitted their bids, digital tools use the answers to present a comprehensive overview of competitors and pricing.

Mass tenders also allow fast analysis of cherry-picking versus consolidation scenarios. Companies can realize savings in one of two ways: They can select many suppliers, cherry-picking so that they choose only the supplier with the lowest price for each particular item. Alternatively, they can consolidate the number of suppliers in the portfolio, being careful to preserve a healthy level of competition. Afterward, companies can use digital analyses to review the existing bids and propose different scenarios. For example, a manufacturer that had a tender with 200 suppliers ran a scenario analysis to learn the maximum number of suppliers that priced at least one line item more cheaply than any other supplier; there were 81. But a different scenario, which looked for the minimum number of suppliers that offered the lowest-priced item, identified 27. Since each of these 27 suppliers bid at least one line item that no other vendor bid on, the manufacturer saw that 27 was the minimum number of suppliers it could have on the tender.

Whenever suppliers do not meet the preset business and regulatory criteria, the platform uses a bidding algorithm to automatically award projects to vendors whose bids meet the original conditions. For more critical events, it can make well-informed suggestions as to which suppliers should be selected. The algorithm systematically "learns" from past auction data to make better recommendations. As a result, the speed and quality of decisions made during bidding and negotiations have improved substantially, now taking days instead of weeks.

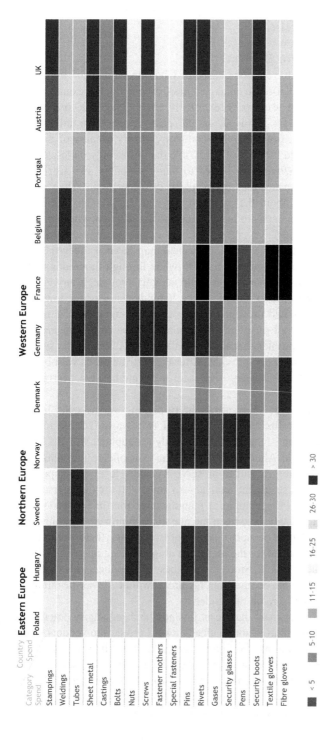

Fig. 4 A heat map provides an overview of where the distributors of different components are located

In addition, companies can use advanced algorithm tools to build a database of bids that suppliers have made in the past and then deploy AI to analyze supplier bidding behavior and predict price changes. These predictions give procurement professionals the information they need to maneuver during negotiations.

Reducing Tail Spend to Extract Value

After setting up tenders and e-auctions, procurement functions can rely on big data, advanced analytics, AI, and automation to reduce whatever tail spend cannot be eliminated. Following the identification of spend patterns with a spend cube, companies can consolidate purchases and suppliers across locations and plants. Advanced analytics and AI can automatically analyze 2D and 3D drawings created by drawing information excellence tools to develop standardized components, and they can also recommend ways to adapt specifications that are not proprietary to any one vendor. For example, there may be a functional reason for the availability of a particular plastic part in different colors; but then again, the colors could simply be decorative. Buyers can now determine themselves whether color really matters for the particular purpose. Such practices can help companies realize economies of scale while shrinking the size of the supplier base. In addition, firms can use advanced analytics to analyze previous purchases and predict demand for the next year. Above that, AI-based instructions to ban spending can be integrated into several digital tools to prohibit spending under certain conditions. For example, a spending ban can be integrated into catalogs to stop purchases once a certain budget limit is reached. AI even allows for more complex governance models that indicate which suppliers are preferred or banned. An additional 1–2% of cost savings are possible.

Looking Ahead

Digital technologies enable an unprecedented level of transparency and management. In the future, companies would be well advised to create a dedicated team that focuses exclusively on tail spend. Procurement employees will need to assess their digital capabilities and create an honest estimate of the value they can create from further digitizing. Truly understanding how large the tail is and how much of it can be managed is prerequisite to creating savings, boosting innovation, ensuring quality and sustainability compliance, and preventing delay and risks in delivery going forward.

Enablers That Make It Work

Generating savings is based on the smart design of the right enabler set. The dimensions of *people* and *performance management* in particular contribute to success with savings. In terms of *people*, it is the right skill set, combining expertise in driving down costs through commercial price negotiations with

(continued)

the technical knowledge needed to be able to challenge specifications. As with the skill set, buyers should be motivated to readily challenge existing specifications internally—not just as a purchaser along the requested specifications. Good buyers are conscious of a company's entire external spend, keeping costs to a minimum. *Performance management* ensures buyers are incentivized to save, but, just as importantly and with clear and rigid guidelines, it secures the validity of cost improvements. What especially needs to be ensured is that only true savings effects are reported. Buyers will neither have the ability to claim windfall effects of any declining markets nor shall they be "blamed" if prices in their market are indeed going up and they are struggling to keep them at lower levels. Furthermore, and based on these guidelines, performance management needs to guarantee that savings are transferred to the P&L statement and budgets. This not only reinforces its credibility toward business partners, it makes the savings stick by adjusted budgets. In addition to people and performance management, the other enabler dimensions play a crucial role in powerful savings generation. In the *organization*, buyers need to be centered in categories with high savings potential and savings generation needs to be a key part of buyers' role descriptions. The *processes* need to clarify primarily how early and with which mandate procurement is to be involved in the development of new products. Last but not least, strong *collaboration* mechanisms between procurement, internal business partners, and suppliers need to be in place and ideally reflected in comprehensive collaboration guidelines. These guidelines may specify how often buyers are to meet with representatives from selected suppliers and how to involve internal business partners in cost-reduction discussions.

Innovation: Finding the Right Partners

The importance of innovation has gone up on the CPO agenda, mostly driven by shorter development cycles, lower value generation, and growing dependency. Not surprisingly, when asked about their top objectives, CPOs rank innovation second, right after cost reductions. According to the Institute for Supply Management, companies that leverage their suppliers' innovative power outperform their peers in top- and bottom-line performance, achieving twice the EBIT, a 5–10% COGS reduction, and a 7–10% revenue boost driven by lower product cost, faster time to market, and higher prices realized.

However, in reality, few companies truly focus on innovation in procurement and therefore fail to deliver on this core value dimension. We analyzed the procurement strategies of 23 different companies. Seven do not mention innovation at all, while another 13 mention it only as an important factor but fail to describe procurement's role and meaning. Only three had a dedicated section on how to deliver supplier innovation, and only one of these three companies involved its business partners in working toward cross-functional value creation.

Starting Position: Procurement Innovation Based on a Company's Strategic Direction

Companies leading in the field of innovation generation combine three core elements in their value generation approach: a clear innovation strategy in procurement, a tailored approach to engage suppliers for innovation, and the smart application of the right innovation levers for suppliers.

The *innovation strategy in procurement* defines the type of innovation needed and is derived from the company's overall innovation ambition. If, for example, a car company wants to lead in UI/UX, this needs to be reflected in procurement's ambition to deliver leading innovation in that field. Therefore, the strategy should translate the company's ambition into a procurement category view, distinguishing between breakthrough and incremental innovation. Breakthrough innovation refers

© Springer Nature Switzerland AG 2020

W. Schnellbächer, D. Weise, *Jumpstart to Digital Procurement*,

https://doi.org/10.1007/978-3-030-51984-1_3

Supplier segmentation yields four clusters of supplier management

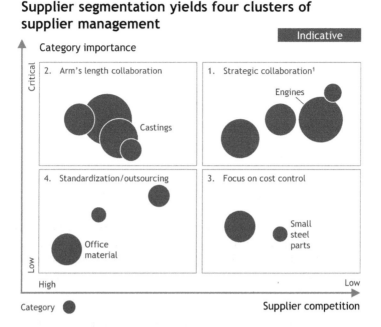

Fig. 1 Engagement approach derived by segmenting categories

to a meaningful change in how to do business and produces a substantial competitive edge. Incremental innovations are small improvements that mostly tackle existing product lines to maintain the competitive position, primarily targeting an improved cost basis. Based on the business partners' needs, a strategy is defined for procurement, distinguishing between categories for breakthrough and incremental innovation.

Along with a clear innovation strategy, leading companies *develop a tailored approach to engage suppliers in innovation*. At first, they leverage the *category importance/supplier competition* matrix and segment categories into different clusters. While *supplier competition* is assessed with regard to competitive intensity in the supply market (from perfect competition to monopoly), the evaluation of *category importance* requires more expert input from other functions, for example, sales. Each cluster implies a different engagement approach. In very competitive supply markets, collaboration needs to be at arm's length. In oligopolistic markets, collaboration should be either strategic or second, or third sources need to be developed (see Fig. 1). If the pool involves a huge number of supplying companies, further clustering is necessary to group suppliers and identify those most suited to strategic partnerships. The companies then combine selected suppliers for joint innovation generation, especially in project-based setups.

The third element for companies is to *build on smart innovation levers*. We distinguish between six levers in our *lever box* and, again, distinguish between breakthrough and incremental innovation (see Fig. 2). While for breakthrough

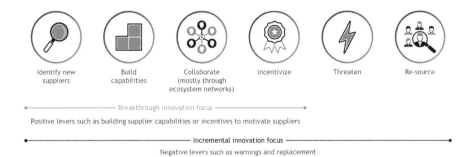

Fig. 2 BCG's innovation lever box

innovation the positive levers such as building supplier capabilities or incentives are crucial, for incremental innovation negative levers such as warnings and replacement can also be used. The reason is simple: While breakthrough ideas cannot be forced, some suppliers hold back incremental innovation to keep margins high. Among the six levers, collaboration through ecosystem networks deserves special attention. Here, suppliers are leveraged in a co-development process. These networks are created with the aim of sourcing ideas from the outside. In the ecosystem, ideas and untapped patents are shared, while a systematic search is made for proven technologies, packages, and products that can be combined, improved, scaled up, and brought to market quickly.

Remaining Challenges

Companies with all three pillars of procurement innovation excellence in place and enablers designed correctly still have a way to go toward completely unlocking procurement's innovation potential. Digital now makes it possible to finally fulfill the promise procurement gives to business partners, namely that it will grant access to the vast innovations in their supplier markets. This promise is to be realized by the following elements:

- Pinpoint suppliers to focus on to receive the best innovation aimed at a given strategic ambition.
- Select the best-suited levers and approaches to motivate strategically chosen suppliers for innovation generation.
- Enhance transparency between the innovation needs of business partners and supplier innovation capabilities.

How Digital Is Changing the Game: Ensuring the Right Suppliers Are Mobilized with the Best-Suited Approach

Pinpoint Suppliers to Focus on to Receive the Best Innovation Targeted to a Given Strategic Ambition

Today, preferred suppliers for joint innovation generation and ecosystems are chosen either according to rules that are too simple (for example, meaningful spend size or total revenue of supplier) or even the buyer's instincts. Breakthrough innovation, however, tends to be found most frequently among smaller niche players—often in high-cost countries. Oftentimes it is exactly those that buyers do not have on their radar for partnerships due to their spend size or initial high-cost situation. Major innovation opportunities are missed because the wrong supplier is selected.

AI innovation coaches tackle this pain point. While the strategy lays out the categories in which innovation is expected, the AI coaches answer which suppliers are likely to deliver innovation. An algorithm runs the data of all suppliers, identifying the probability of future innovation. To do that, it analyzes input factors such as the supplier size and location, parameters on their R&D function, the total and relative share of R&D spend, the number of patents, the quality of the relationship, or the supplier's financial stability. The supplier selection algorithms usually run with around 20–30 input parameters. After the necessary data is defined, collection from external and internal sources can start. Internal data might be pulled from fragmented repositories (e.g., the business warehouse), from local data sources in plants, or remote data files. Information from these sources is required to assess the innovative potential of suppliers based on their product design. The challenge with external data is to identify the source of the requisite information. While market reports and industry outlooks are publically available, supplier-specific information (e.g., on financial stability, R&D expenditures, the number of patents) needs to be requested from the supplier through RfIs. Openly communicating the connection between the request and the overall innovation initiative to the suppliers is key to success.

Select the Best-Suited Levers and Approaches to Motivate Strategically Chosen Suppliers for Innovation Generation

Even when preferred suppliers are chosen, it is often unclear how best to motivate them to generate and share innovations. Again, AI can be leveraged to choose the most powerful lever for each situation by picking it from the six-lever box introduced above. The data used for the supplier selection algorithm is used as a starting point because the supplier's size has a strong effect on which lever is most motivational, for example. However, it is enhanced with more internal information, such as the trust in the relationship or the power ratio (e.g., relative share of spend versus suppliers' revenue, the supplier's industries growth). Based on this, another

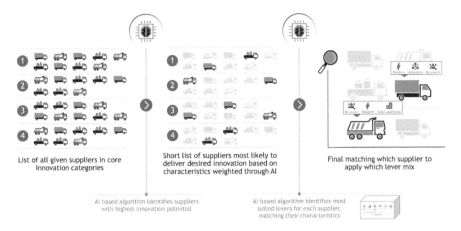

List of all given suppliers in core Innovation categories

Short list of suppliers most likely to deliver desired innovation based on characteristics weighted through AI

Final matching which supplier to apply which lever mix

AI based algorithm identifies suppliers with highest innovation potential

AI based algorithm identifies most suited levers for each supplier, matching their characteristics

Fig. 3 Illustration of AI-based innovation selection

algorithm then determines whether a supplier should build capabilities and be incentivized, or whether it might be more effective to demand incremental cost innovation using threats (see Fig. 3).

Two crucial points should be made about both innovation coaches: the one for supplier selection and the one for choosing the right innovation levers. Initially, all AI-based recommendations are no more than that—recommendations. The final call is still made by the respective buyer. The most crucial input for AI-based learning is feedback from the buyers regarding how successful supplier and lever selection was in terms of realized power. Here it is normally sufficient to enter whether the buyer followed the innovation coach's recommendation or chose a different supplier or lever. In addition, the success of innovation is to be reported as a predefined KPI or a KPI set. The coach can then review how good each of its recommendations has been and, based on the input, constantly improve its algorithm over time.

How It Has Been Done: AI-Based Supplier Innovation at an Automotive OEM

A global automotive OEM had outsourced about 70% of the parts of the overall vehicle. Based on that heavy dependency, a focus group was created to better enable incremental innovation for its suppliers. The group started with a deep-dive analysis on a sample parts catalog covering tubes, stamped parts, fasteners, and large motor components, and the results were devastating.

- *The supplier commitments to bring long-term efficiency gains and reduce prices over time had largely been "baked" into prices from the start.*
- *If suppliers had experienced innovation breakthroughs, they had kept them to themselves without letting the automotive OEM know about them in order to protect their margins.*

(continued)

- *Overall, there was little to no transparency on either the true innovation potential of suppliers or the innovations they had truly succeeded in achieving in the past.*

As a consequence, the management decided to leverage a comprehensive digital approach to suppliers' innovation generation, in which an AI-based algorithm was applied to a portfolio of close to 1100 suppliers in the target categories. The results of this algorithm were matched with an assessment by the respective category buyers of which suppliers they felt were the most promising. The resulting supplier lists of both approaches showed an overlap of 83% and were combined into a list of 100 innovation leaders. An assessment was subsequently run on the selected sample as to which supplier might be especially receptive to what mix of innovation levers based on the six-element innovation toolbox. The buyers therefore had clarity not only on which suppliers to focus on to drive innovation but also on the combination of tools to use with which supplier. This tool combination was seen as a recommendation rather than a binding order, yet in most cases the buyers appreciated the AI-based guidance and happily followed it. In the 6 months following the push, the function experienced a price drop of 2% above long-term agreements, with an additional 4% promised for the coming 18 months. The CPO was especially surprised that incremental innovation was possible in technologies he perceived as standard and fully optimized, such as the press speed, coil-change time, or scrap usage in stamped parts.

Enhance Transparency Between Innovation Needs of Business Partners and Supplier Innovation Capabilities

Finally, in the past, buyers struggled to manage the collaboration between suppliers, internal business partners, and procurement itself. Typically, only infrequent discussions were organized to exchange ideas. Yet there was no continuous exchanging of ideas and it has often not been transparent for suppliers what the engineering or R&D unit of the buying company is working on and vice versa. This challenge is tackled through *collaboration platforms*. On the one hand, these ensure transparency along the development process through continued information sharing and thus represent a key element in creating trust. On the other hand, they act as a platform for organizing joint work procedures. Joint tasks are given, ideas generated, and each function sees the different projects and initiatives the supplying or buying company is working on at the moment. A special type of innovation platform is the open ones in which many suppliers, including those along the supply chain, can participate. Such open platforms are generally used in the early stages of innovation generation, including upfront supplier selection. When projects become more mature, only selected suppliers will be connected directly with the buying companies' engineering function. Either only a tier 1 supplier or also their respective suppliers (that is, tier 2 from the view of the buying company) are involved in joint idea generation.

Looking Ahead

Digital directly tackles those challenges that keep buying companies from successfully leveraging supplier innovation. Using the right tools, buyers are able to pick the most innovative suppliers as partners, find the right incentive mechanism for each of these suppliers, and connect the value generation units from suppliers and their company in powerful collaboration platforms.

Enablers That Make It Work

A strong focus on these three pillars alone, however, doesn't lead to excellence in procurement innovation. Particularly *processes* and *collaboration* are of key importance. In the field of *processes*, product development needs to be differentiated from operational procure-to-pay.

- Product development: Procurement has to be involved early to reflect the impact of product development decisions on the sourcing opportunities and the supplier's ability to contribute to innovation; and second, procurement can keep preferred suppliers in the loop regarding upcoming innovations. Generally, suppliers have deep insight into upcoming technologies and understand the needs of customers and competitors. By partnering with key strategic suppliers, procurement secures access to the technology advantage and market know-how that is critical for new product development. Leaders in procurement establish an innovation radar and scout for innovative suppliers and future technologies, which ensures agility in identifying needs and bringing innovations to market.
- Procure-to-pay: The P2P focus has to be adapted to different category requirements. In fast-track categories with a high innovation need, purchase order approvals should be speeded up. In a competitive landscape, innovative suppliers diligently choose the introduction of innovation. Treating innovative suppliers well should therefore be a top priority.

In terms of *collaboration*, it is crucial to define clear guidelines on joint working procedures for suppliers and internal business partners. Collaboration needs to be founded on trust and a strong business relationship. We found especially powerful collaboration models between procurement and business partners that are located in the same buildings with suppliers sitting in the same

(continued)

region. If suppliers and business partners who are not co-located are chosen for collaboration, the company needs to ensure that the distance is bridged by regular face-to-face visits for the developing groups or virtual meetings are empowered by a digital collaboration platform. For business partners and suppliers, these meetings should become a focused KPI.

Other enablers also need to be designed to ensure an innovation-focused function. The categories defined as "focus" in the innovation strategy need to be sufficiently equipped with resources in the organization. Likewise, buyers' capabilities in the *people* dimension need to be tailored in focus categories. In categories where breakthrough innovation is crucial, buyers should be trained to detect a supplier's innovation potential, search for new suppliers, and build a supplier ecosystem. In categories where incremental innovation is key, buyers need to be properly equipped with the technical know-how to challenge existing production procedures. To encourage the right behavior internally and from suppliers, the right *performance management* setup needs to be inherent in KPIs and incentives. Again, we differentiate between breakthrough and incremental innovation. In breakthrough innovation, KPIs are the number of new ideas from suppliers, of patents jointly developed, and revenue growth. In incremental innovation, the focus is more on cost improvements achieved jointly through technical ideas and delivery/quality improvements. These KPIs should be complemented by the business partners' satisfaction with the innovation delivered by procurement. This ensures that procurement actions serve the business needs rather than merely fulfilling KPIs.

Quality: Highlighting What Is Actually Delivered

The need to obtain high-quality products and services from suppliers has never been greater. Failures increase costs (for example, in the form of warranty claims, product recalls, and lawsuits) and damage revenue and branding irrevocably. Best-in-class companies have used a variety of practices to mitigate and smartly prevent quality failures across the supply chain. They have focused on identifying which components require the highest quality, where quality issues have occurred and are likely to occur, and how to best reduce the risk of failures in the future.

Digital technologies have the potential to boost procurement's quality management to a new level. Big data, advanced analytics, artificial intelligence, and collaborative platforms provide a high degree of precision, and they enable companies to predict and mitigate quality failures much more effectively than in the past. Estimates show that deploying digital solutions can reduce procurement quality issues by as much as 60–70%.

Starting Position: Not Even Knowing Where Quality Is Needed

Best-in-class companies follow a three-step approach to ensure that they have the right components of the right quality on hand to create the products and services that meet their customers' needs: First, they determine where quality is most needed. Second, they pinpoint where product failures occur. Third, they mitigate known risks of quality failure.

When trying to (1) *determine where quality is most needed*, most companies have to admit that they do not have the resources required to give every product in their portfolio the same attention. Best-in-class companies, therefore, cluster their products along two dimensions (see Fig. 1):

- Strategic importance (i.e., the value that the component provides to customers)
- Required quality level (ranging from the minimum industry standard to a premier level usually associated with innovative offerings)

© Springer Nature Switzerland AG 2020

W. Schnellbächer, D. Weise, *Jumpstart to Digital Procurement*,
https://doi.org/10.1007/978-3-030-51984-1_4

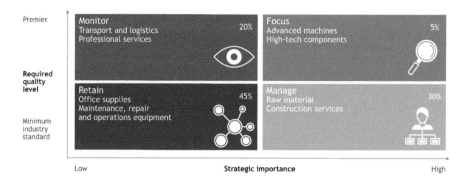

Fig. 1 The quality assessment matrix pinpoints where to focus quality efforts

We added sample categories that are naturally highly dependent on the industry as well as the individual company strategy.

However, even with the right clustering method in place, best-in-class procurement teams still struggle to put the right quality requirements in place for their focus products. Typically, other functions—mostly sales and operations—claim responsibility for determining the necessary quality requirements and, frequently, they do so without explicitly considering cost or value created. As a result, the bar can be set too high, for example, when road transports are handled as dangerous goods whether or not they need this level of care, or too low, which may mean disappointed customers. In either case, the procurement function is limited in its ability to challenge these requirements even if it has the capacity to specify quality requirements for the most important products and services purchased.

When (2) *pinpointing where product failures occur* in the supply chain, leading companies rely on frameworks (for example, the eight disciplines of problem-solving or the five whys) to determine the root cause of a defect. Moreover, they use multivariate analyses to monitor the quality of those components that must be of the highest quality. However, while these frameworks are useful, they do not go far enough. Even when they help trace a failure back to a particular supplier, they do not determine the reason for that failure. Limitations also apply to multivariate analyses. They can help to identify the causes of quality problems for high-quality components, however, they overlook defects in those of lower quality. Also, quality detection is typically retrospective and based on the assumption that future quality failures are likely to occur where failures have happened in the past. But as product portfolios change more and more rapidly, this assumption is becoming less valid.

When (3) *mitigating risks of quality failure*, leading companies typically use the information gathered in (1) and (2) to determine procurement's optimal point of involvement in the product and service life cycle as well as the quality levers that should be applied in the respective stage. Products and services developed jointly with suppliers require proactive, early-stage mitigation, while reactive measures are sufficient for less important ones (see Fig. 2). This proactive-reactive approach has

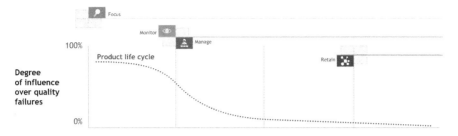

Fig. 2 Conventional levers address quality issues throughout the product life cycle

its merits but is also labor intensive when considering the thousands of goods and services usually procured.

Remaining Challenges

Despite all the efforts in quality management, only a few companies can claim to truly excel in this value dimension. Digital tools can raise procurement's quality management to a whole new level by providing solutions to the challenges that remain:

- Understand where quality matters most.
- Identify where quality problems occur throughout the supply chain and even predict upcoming failures.
- Allow companies to take the most appropriate actions to mitigate failures in the future.

How Digital Is Changing the Game: Making The Fragmentation Manageable

Understand Where Quality Matters Most

Collaborative platforms and advanced analytics are critical for determining the quality requirements for all components and services no matter where they are located in the quality matrix. Collaborative platforms facilitate the communication between business partners and they process and archive all documents that are exchanged. They connect customer requirements to internal production and further drive the information through procurement into the entire supply chain. Advanced analytics can then help to assess the data from these evaluations and determine the right quality level for each product in the matrix. These assessments are also useful for scenario analyses, for example, to understand the role that each part of a car seat plays in protecting a baby in different kinds of car accidents.

How It Has Been Done: Quality Management at a Fast-Food Producer

A large burger chain's procurement team performed a conjoint analysis with more than 2000 consumers to determine what mattered the most in terms of the burger's taste—the beef, lettuce, bun, ketchup, onions, or tomato. The group used advanced analytics to assess the value that each component delivered relative to the overall cost of the burger. It also analyzed the standard deviation of the quality of products procured from suppliers. The bun turned out to be the second most important part of the burger but, at the same time, the analysis revealed large inconsistencies in terms of quality. This feedback helped the burger chain shift its attention toward bun quality, which led to much greater customer satisfaction.

Once companies have a good understanding of where quality is important, they can formulate KPIs and service level agreements for all products and services in the matrix. Having such requirements allows the procurement team to question internal stakeholders who want to use different metrics.

Identify Where Quality Problems Occur Throughout the Supply Chain and Even Predict Upcoming Failures

After creating a more precise view of where quality is needed and what level is required, companies can use digital tools to consolidate information from various data sources to create a comprehensive overview of the supply chain. This data is generated automatically (for example, from statements containing quality claims that are produced when parts are delivered to a plant) and complemented with information from the staff in the receiving function who accept and approve incoming goods and services using an app on their smartphone. This input includes other details, such as which products and services arrived late or were in need of quality adjustments. An augmented reality app is especially useful in this context as it facilitates the evaluation of a product's weight, material, density, and inner contents. Companies can also ask their suppliers to use such apps to assess their own products before shipping. These technologies are typically used in conjunction with a dashboard that can constantly analyze data from the different channels and provide an overview for procurement, internal business partners, and suppliers alike.

Once the information on the incoming products is combined with other data, such as invoices, quality reports, and supplier balance sheets, AI algorithms can predict where the next quality failure is likely to occur. They weigh different data points and information learned from past experience to generate a short list of the suppliers and components that are most likely to experience quality failures. Typical data points at supplier level might be their industry, size in terms of revenue, relative spend with the buying company toward the total sales, their production location, number of FTE in quality, or simply their history of quality failures if this has been recorded. At a company level, the supplier information of the delivering company is enhanced with data such as the component volume, complexity, type, or volatility in demand, which has proven to be one of the key drivers of quality failures. AI is now taking these algorithms and refining them over time. For every quality failure—forecasted or not—in a given scenario, the algorithm is better able to rate the parameters used and therefore enhance the credibility of its projections.

How It Has Been Done: Quality Management at a Chemicals Manufacturer

A chemicals manufacturer recently installed a system that can predict where in the company's vast portfolio quality is likely to drop. The algorithm consistently listed 20–50 parts (out of 3000) that merited closer monitoring. Over a 12-month period, the system predicted quality failures with more than 80% accuracy. To do so, the algorithm rated 22 variables (e.g., the trend in internal quality feedback, past quality problems, the size and location of each supplier). Some of the most influential factors came as a surprise. For example, invoices sent substantially earlier than usual revealed that a supplier was in financial distress. And it turned out that these suppliers were highly likely to be responsible for some of the quality failures. Acting on insights like these, the company reduced quality problems by 51%.

Allow Companies to Take the Most Appropriate Actions to Mitigate Failures in the Future

When it comes to using levers to mitigate quality failures, digital solutions offer two main advantages. First, they expand the number of actions companies can take to reduce problems and, second, it provides guidance on which levers to apply in which situations.

Digital levers can be used to reduce the risk of quality failures throughout the product and service life cycle. Supplier collaboration platforms, for example, greatly facilitate joint efforts with suppliers in the concept phase, while sensors make it easier to collect and assess relevant performance data in the supplier management phase (see Fig. 3). In one example, a chemicals producer discovered that some of its raw material input contained traces of a different material. An analysis revealed that the contamination took place during transport: the logistics provider had not cleaned the silo trailers sufficiently after transporting another material. The manufacturer added KPIs to its logistics contracts to spell out the cleaning requirements. And it installed dedicated sensors in the plant to monitor the quality of inbound materials and a quality-tracking and response system to compare the results with the KPIs. These technologies allowed the company to reject full truckloads right at the point of unloading in cases where the supplier did not meet the KPIs. The system also

	Concept	Strategy creation	Supplier selection	Supplier management
Conventional quality levers	Complexity reduction	Minimum product standards definition	New-supplier development and audit	Existing-supplier development and audit
	Joint product development	Minimum supplier standards definition	Reference list at component level	Supplier quality engineer rapid-response team
	Concept competition focusing on quality	Number of suppliers, from dual to multiple sourcing	Incentive design linked to qualitative performance	Intermediate system testing
	Early technology incubation	Escalation procedures	Supplier contingency plan	Consequence management
Digitally enhanced quality levers	Supplier collaboration platforms	AA-powered supplier feedback loops	Automated contract setup and management	Dashboard for quality monitoring
	Best-practice exchange platforms	Lesson learned from big data that allow for correct design from the outset	Internal and external data on previous warranty issues	Supply chain control tower for intelligent forecasting
	Online innovation contests	Automated total cost of ownership calculation	Intelligent supplier scouting	Automated claims management
	Predictive analytics on future quality requirements	Risk assessment enabled by big data	Blockchain-enabled transparency on supplier performance	Automated and sensor assessed inbound quality

Fig. 3 Conventional and digitally enhanced quality levers help mitigate quality failures

allowed the buyer to expedite claims against the supplier and manage the relationship more effectively.

Digital tools can also guide buyers as to which lever—conventional or digital—is the most effective in the purchasing situation at hand. For example, for individual and advanced production machinery, the best lever might be online innovation contests, while for maintenance, repair, and operations (MRO) parts, automated claims management might be beneficial. Again AI plays a key role. Just as we have seen with AI negotiation coaches, algorithms can select the lever best suited to each purchasing situation. Is it better to threaten the supplier with quality claims or rather build his capabilities? Or is resourcing the best option? The algorithms scan past actions and their impact on quality performance in a given situation and therefore suggest the best-suited lever. Just as in the AI negotiation coaches, the recommendations the algorithm makes are nonbinding. Using big data and learning from the past, the algorithm can perceive not only where quality failures may occur but how to prevent them. Buyers can base their decisions on this information. Over time, the algorithm learns which levers are the most powerful in each situation and continually improves its recommendations.

Looking Ahead

Digital technologies will be crucial for defining, monitoring, and improving the quality of products and services going forward. However, to leverage these technologies in the best possible way, procurement must challenge its current quality management approaches to identify apparent issues and create a prioritized digital agenda. That payoff can be substantial: Companies that use digital technologies to their fullest potential stand to improve the quality of their input while increasing revenue, reducing costs, and boosting innovation.

Enablers That Make It Work

Using the right digital tools in the right situations does not necessarily guarantee success. To realize the full benefit, the supporting elements must be in place. In particular, four enablers stand out: *processes*, *people*, *performance management*, and *collaboration*.

First, quality management needs to be deeply embedded in the sourcing *processes*. This is particularly critical for key categories. In source-to-contract (S2C) processes, which start with defining individual projects and their needs and end with the signing of supplier contracts, quality requirements for suppliers should already be embedded in the category strategies. In procure-to-pay (P2P) processes, which begin with the decision to buy a good or service and end with delivery and payment, technical quality tests should be used in situations where only one supplier is involved.

(continued)

Second, companies should create a quality management team made up of digitally skilled *people* from procurement and other functions to deal with quality issues proactively. In contrast with existing continuous-improvement teams that mainly fix problems once they arise, this team would use predictive analytics to (a) understand where quality is most important and (b) resolve potential quality failures in conjunction with suppliers before they even occur. In addition, companies should implement training programs to teach procurement employees how to leverage digital tools for quality management. These training courses are neither limited to the procurement function nor to one's own company.

Third, companies should measure their employees in procurement and in quality department, those working with suppliers and the suppliers themselves against the same quality goals in their *performance management*. While this clearly represents a departure from conventional practice—procurement teams usually don't include supplier quality in performance management efforts— our experience has shown that high-performing suppliers can help reduce the total cost of ownership.

Last not least, business partners also need to be onboarded, for example, showing how their *collaboration* is needed for preventive or reactive quality levers—be they digital or not. Suppliers need to be shown what data they need to provide and how they are to react to varying quality standards over time. A 360° training approach ensures that all relevant stakeholders are addressed and equipped with the right capabilities.

Sustainability: Adding Sustainability as Procurement's New Value Proposition

Sustainability is increasingly gaining in importance for companies in general and procurement functions in particular. With extreme weather and natural disasters occurring more frequently across the globe and youth movements calling for us all to act now to save the planet, environmental protection is becoming a core task. Of equally increasing importance are a company's social impact and ethical standards. Together these factors are broadly known as environmental, social, and governance (ESG) factors. Governments are increasing the pressure by issuing more sustainability-related regulations (e.g., the UK's Modern Slavery Act and the CSR Directive Implementation Act in Germany). Furthermore, the market stakeholders, such as investors and customers, are demanding that companies focus more of their attention on ensuring sustainability. According to a recent "BCG Pulse of the Fashion Industry" update, 75% of consumers surveyed consider sustainability as extremely important or very important. And, more than 50% of consumers plan to switch brands in the future if another brand acts more environmentally and socially friendly than their preferred one.

The requirement to ensure sustainability extends beyond the companies themselves and penetrates the entire supply chain. Neglecting sustainability issues in the supply network can have an immediate and disastrous effect, such as deteriorating customer perception where suppliers act unethically. As the point of contact linking companies with their supply chain, procurement must play the core role of supporting the company in maintaining a high sustainability standard across the supply chain and in fulfilling the rising customer demands on sustainable products on an ongoing basis.

© Springer Nature Switzerland AG 2020
W. Schnellbächer, D. Weise, *Jumpstart to Digital Procurement*,
https://doi.org/10.1007/978-3-030-51984-1_5

Starting Position: Anchoring Sustainability in the Procurement Setup

Best-in-class companies across different industries that have successfully anchored sustainability in their procurement setup share three characteristics: They *define sustainability and the impact the company can have on it from the start*, they *embed it visibly into the procurement processes*, and they *apply appropriate levers to mitigate sustainability issues*.

First, it is important to ensure the *right definition of sustainability* and describe the direct impact a company and especially its procurement function can have. There are three sustainability dimensions: (1) *Environmental*, describing the aim of keeping in balance all of the earth's environmental systems while at the same time consuming natural resources only at the rate at which they can replenish themselves. Here, outcomes such as the carbon footprint of a company or the impact on clean water play a key role. (2) *Economical*, describing how human communities across the globe will be able to meet their needs through a circular and intact system. (3) *Social*, aiming for all people throughout the world to be treated in accordance with universal human rights and for them to have access to sufficient resources in order to keep their families and communities healthy and secure. A company has to clearly identify the impact its supply chain has on these three sustainability dimensions and how it makes that impact. Take, for example, a French manufacturer of construction material with only local supply of such as sand or engineering services and, at the same time, high energy consumption with large CO_2 emissions. Procurement here should focus on new technologies for reducing this CO_2 footprint and therefore emphasize the environmental sustainability dimension. A fashion producer with a complex supply chain in Asia, on the other hand, very likely has to pay more particular attention to the economic and social sustainability dimension.

Second the sustainability ambition needs to be *embedded visibly into procurement processes*. As elaborated in the section on "speed," procurement activities fall into three main categories. The sustainability elements should be embedded end to end into all three sub-processes, from strategy design to daily purchasing (see Fig. 1).

In the *planning-to-strategy (P2S)* process, the definition of the procurement strategy and targets should be aligned with the business strategy as well as the sustainability vision of the company. To better steer and track procurement performance in achieving sustainability targets, ESG-related KPIs are derived and incorporated into an overall procurement performance framework. As achievement of these targets demands strong support from and close collaboration with suppliers, the strategy and targets for sustainable procurement are clearly communicated throughout the entire supply network. For example, the global agricultural equipment manufacturer AGCO stated in its procurement mission statement that they urge their supplier network to "deliver sustainable quality and value" in all their products and services. Unilever, the international consumer goods company, published on their website their target of sourcing 100% of agricultural raw materials in a sustainable way.

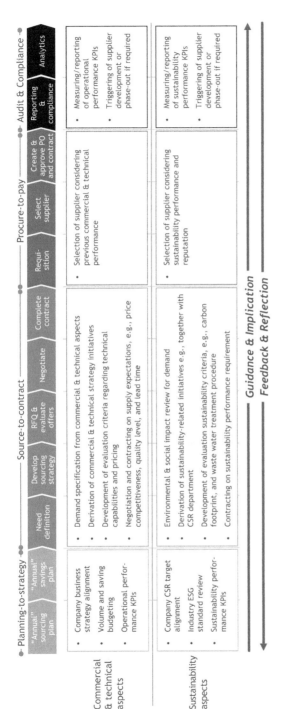

Fig. 1 Embedding sustainability into procurement process

To translate the sustainability vision and targets into procurement operation, it is necessary to derive the implications of the vision and targets and have them reflected through the *source-to-contract (S2C)* process. It starts by considering the potential environmental impact in the demand specification (e.g., usage of nontoxic materials in production) and extends to incorporating ESG criteria (e.g., carbon footprint or chemicals treatment) into an evaluation matrix for tendering and negotiation. Best-in-class companies go one step further and treat the fulfillment of sustainability standards as the knockout criteria when commissioning suppliers. Agreement on sustainability requirements and targets is laid down in contractual terms to provide a solid reference basis for both parties.

In day-to-day operations in the *procure-to-pay (P2P)* process, the suppliers' sustainability record is considered along with their commercial and technical performance (such as pricing, quality level, and innovation potential) during actual purchasing and supplier selection. The best rating companies obligate the involvement and approval of the companies' CSR departments if a supplier showing inferior sustainability performance has to be selected due to other limitations, such as capacity availability or the technical specification.

The performance of the suppliers and procurement in terms of sustainability is continuously measured against predefined targets. Any gaps or any risks of not meeting the targets are immediately reported to management so that countermeasures can be launched in good time. Regular communication of good performance, such as target overachievement, is equally important to gaining momentum and to motivate further contribution to the sustainability vision.

How It Has Been Done: Sustainable Sourcing at a Global Leading Brewing Company

A brewing company with more than 200 brands in its portfolio had to heavily source agricultural raw materials. With a growing world population and increasing demand for those raw materials, ensuring increased productivity in a sustainable way was crucial not only to securing supply but also to protecting the brand image. However, it was a huge challenge with a supplier base spanning over 100 countries. To achieve the sustainability goals, the company integrated a four-layer process into their procurement framework. First, all suppliers were required to sign a Supplier Code that provided clear guidance on and the expectations for fulfilling sustainability standards. Before onboarding new suppliers, an internal analysis was conducted and focused on potential sustainability threats related to the purchased category and the countries in which the suppliers were located. Those suppliers flagged as high threat had to undergo a more comprehensive assessment. To do so, the company collaborated with a service provider and developed a specific supplier questionnaire and scoring models. If the rating fell below the company's minimum threshold, a third party site audit using a standard

(continued)

> *industry protocol was triggered. This process was first implemented for its 150 strategic suppliers and was then rolled out on a global basis. One year later, 34% of agricultural raw materials were sourced from sustainable sources and 95% of suppliers showed compliance with the Supplier Code. This achievement was highly recognized by transnational organizations such as the European Cooperative for Rural Development (EUCORD).*

Lastly, companies must *apply appropriate levers to mitigate sustainability issues.* Unlike risk events that cause direct financial loss, sustainability issues can lead to a loss of reputation. They can, however, also endanger a company's long-term or even mid-term financial performance if not quickly and properly handled. For example, a German conglomerate was excluded for months from participating in public tenders for the Norwegian state grid operator because one of its suppliers in Eastern Europe was accused of paying unfair wages to employees.

Therefore, a variety of sustainability issues must be constantly tracked, reported, and dealt with by selecting and applying the optimal levers. Similar to risk management levers, the levers ensuring sustainability can be categorized into three clusters (see Fig. 2). The *transparency* lever thoroughly screens potential sustainability issues to grant visibility into potential subjects that could harm a company's reputation; for example, by incorporating ESG-related questions into supplier on-site auditing to ensure compliance with all applicable sustainability standards. While the *preventive ensuring* lever minimizes or prevents sustainability incidences, the *reactive ensuring* lever reduces the brand damage caused by any sustainability issues that have already occurred. As social media becomes more popular and consumers are increasingly sustainability-conscious, any news of toxic water pollution or child labor, for example, can spread rapidly and do unrevokable damage to the company's reputation even when the company makes use of reactive levers, such as publically severing ties with suppliers demonstrating unethical behavior. Thus preventive levers are preferred to reactive ones.

Fig. 2 Illustrative selection of sustainability ensuring levers

How It Has Been Done: Implementation of a Detox Program at a Leading German Supermarket Chain

As a well-known grocery chain selling household and health-related products, a German supermarket chain was under the steady scrutiny of its customers as it sought to secure safety and sustainability in the supply chain; for example, low to no use of hazardous chemicals in the production of textiles. To establish better transparency and prevent the occurrence of brand-damaging incidents, the company joined the Detox Campaign and implemented a group-wide program targeting a toxic-free supply chain. As part of the program, various levers were applied in a joint effort with third-party service providers and suppliers. For example, suppliers participating in the tendering process were obligated to name all the supply chain partners contributing to the production of their textiles so that sustainability along the supply chain could be screened. The waste water from production was tested against detox requirements on an annual basis. If any non-compliance was identified, the suppliers were given a very rigid time frame in which to correct the issue and were to be phased out if they did not manage to fulfill the detox requirements again. To support its suppliers in achieving the goals, targeted training sessions were rolled out worldwide. For example, 20 supplier training courses were held in China and Bangladesh and the suppliers' performance in chemicals management in production was improved by 27%.

Remaining Challenges

As this is a new value dimension for procurement, there is as yet little experience of data-based decision-making and action-taking with regards to ensuring sustainability in procurement. With the supply chain becoming more global and complex and regulatory bodies and customers assigning more responsibilities to buy companies when it comes to maintaining high sustainability standards in their supply network, the conventional best-in-class approach is slowly reaching its limit. New digital technologies are emerging and can support procurement in addressing two major challenges in particular:

- Revealing the hidden threat through data mining
- Building trust over complex supply chains

How Digital Is Changing the Game: Bringing Facts and Visibility to an Intransparent Supply Chain

Revealing the Hidden Threat Through Data Mining

Evaluation of sustainability performance across the supply chain and identification of potential threats both involve collecting and processing enormous amounts of data, not only from the suppliers themselves but also from the environment and society in which the suppliers are active. While some of the data and information can be easily extracted from a company's own or their suppliers' ERP systems, other relevant data has to be acquired from a variety of sources. For example, government websites have to be regularly visited to keep up to date with newly issued regulations; the scientific database has to be routinely checked to see if any production approach has recently proven harmful to our health; social media must be continuously screened to ensure awareness of any arising sustainability campaign for or against certain activities in the supply chain. None of these tasks can be managed if done manually. Big data technology has the power to compile all the required data from different sources, to structure the logic and links between them, and to present users with the outcome in a lean and target-oriented manner.

Moreover, big data combined with AI provides advanced intelligence that reveals the hidden facts and can predict trends in sustainable supply chain management. In complicated product development, for example, the buying companies purchase integrated modules from tier-1 suppliers that assemble the parts sourced from multiple upstream sub-suppliers. The potential sustainability threats rooted in tier-2 or tier-3 suppliers could be easily overlooked if buying companies focus only on the tier-1 level. Also at the impact quantification stage, the potential business damage could be underestimated due to low purchasing volumes in a category, notwithstanding the fact that this category is used in all major end products. Digital technologies draw all the pieces of information together into one big picture so that the potential threat and actual impact can be accurately and thoroughly evaluated.

> **How It Has Been Done: Sustainability Threat Monitoring at a Chemicals Producer**
>
> *A European chemicals producer focused the attention it paid to threat prevention solely on bankruptcies, especially of smaller suppliers, and the subsequent shortages within the supply chain. However, when the Chinese government began closing plants for environmental reasons, the CPO was worried about hidden sustainability threats and requested an assessment of direct products sourced from China. The results were shocking: Around 60% of the company's end products contained an ingredient made in China and were therefore exposed to this new threat. Despite the fact that no Chinese*

(continued)

supplier had faced bankruptcy in the past, the supply security could have been endangered as a result of sudden plant closures for environmental reasons.

At first, a conventional assessment was plotted for the main materials, weighing the probability of a plant closure against the impact on the company's end products, with the input parameters for the assessed probability incidents being chosen from the same industry. Of 1800 raw materials sourced from China, a total of 500 were rated as high threat based on high probability combined with sizeable impact. More sophisticated monitoring was required. A sustainability management database was therefore set up that combined a large amount of internal as well as external information, ranging from the suppliers' quality reports, location, size, and invoice timing through press reports about closures in the same industry and region, or changes in local governments with a different environmental focus. Building on that database, an AI-aided algorithm was introduced that regularly scanned all known Chinese suppliers for a potential plant closure. The algorithm consisted of 23 input parameters based on the big data source and took into account closures that had already taken place in the industry. Based on that information, it refined its results over time. Search bots automatically searched through the external information and fed it into the algorithms. The algorithms identified a subsample of around 55 materials exposed to high threat—something that could be monitored much more easily than the 500 in the original cluster. After a year, two plants were actually closed—both of which were in the closely monitored subsample.

Building Trust Over Complex Supply Chains

Blockchain ensures good traceability throughout the supply chain, helping companies to ensure compliance with environmental and ethical standards, among other things. For example, companies need to prove they are avoiding conflict resources, hazardous materials, and child labor, and they also want proof of green energy usage, rain forest certificates, etc. In the past, data sources were easily corrupted by manipulation, making data unreliable throughout the supply chain. Blockchain eliminates this issue by providing a safe environment in which a network of computers ensures validation and the authenticity of data. Furthermore, it integrates data along the supply chain to increase transparency between nodes, which makes traceability effective and trustworthy.

A recent example is a collaborative digital platform developed to help one of the world's largest diamond companies to securely track diamonds throughout the value chain and ensure ethical origins. The platform integrates data from various stakeholders, including producers, governments, banks, graders, retailers, and traders in one consolidated system. As the diamond passes through the value chain, the systems verifies and stores transactions to create a clear string of information. By storing information on size, color, and certificates, the platform gives owners confidence about the origin of their diamond.

Looking Ahead

Procurement has only begun to harness the significantly greater possibilities for value generation in sustainability. Unlike cost reductions and efficiency improvement that can be directly or even immediately reflected in P&L reporting, value created by optimal sustainability performance is hard to recognize from a financial perspective and only over a long period of time. This requires persistence on the part of procurement and enduring commitment from all business partners. To ensure transparency and build trust across the supply chain, big data and digital tools can be leveraged to support the procurement team. With the further development of technologies, more use cases can be identified for facilitating implementation of a sustainable supply chain and for transforming it into a new competitive factor for the business.

Enablers That Make It Work

Ensuring sustainability in the supply chain is not a one-off initiative but involves an ongoing change in mindset and behavior when purchasing goods and services. Two enabler dimensions in particular, *process* and *collaboration*, play a crucial role in enabling this transformational change. The procurement *process* has to shift from focusing only on the commercial and technical side to also considering sustainability aspects. Under certain circumstances, this shift can cause conflict between the different value dimensions. Additional sustainability assessments, for example, may slow down process speed, while selecting suppliers with better sustainability records can impair the achievement of savings targets. Procurement must work closely with both internal and external business partners in order to optimally balance sustainability with other value dimensions. Through *collaboration* with other functions as well as suppliers, the importance of sustainability is clearly transmitted, equally acknowledged, and ensures constant commitment from all stakeholders across the entire supply chain.

The other enabler dimensions are also important for facilitating ongoing change. A corresponding *organization* design should be in place and *people* in the procurement team must be equipped with the necessary mindset and expertise. The consideration of sustainability factors has to be embedded in the procurement strategy and role profiles of different levers, from CPO to buyers. Regular training sessions are organized not only to reconsolidate the focus on sustainability but also to update all stakeholders on the most recent

(continued)

amendments, such as new environmental regulations or social campaigns. To retain the commitment of stakeholders and maintain the momentum, target achievement status and success stories have to be measured and reported to all contributing parties on an ongoing basis through a structured *performance management* framework.

Speed: Leveraging Bots as Our New Best Friends

As business cycles quicken, procurement functions are under pressure to purchase goods and services faster than ever. Digital technologies make it possible to accelerate the procurement process that begins with the need to buy an item or service and ends with payment and delivery. According to our estimate, the time required can drop by as much as 80% for simple items like office supplies and 40% for complex technical items like capital projects.

Given the vast possibilities for addressing this issue, many companies are at a loss as to how to create a speedy and user-friendly setup that will stick. We have found that a combination of traditional and digital methods yields the best results. Tackled correctly, a significant speed boost in procurement is possible with limited effort. The key considerations to be borne in mind are the following.

Starting Position: Ensuring a Lean Setup

Procurement activities fall into three main categories.

- *Planning-to-strategy (P2S)*—strategic processes that begin with planning the procurement process and end with defining the category strategy.
- *Source-to-contract (S2C)*—operational processes that start with defining individual projects and their needs and end with signing supplier contracts.
- *Procure-to-pay (P2P)*—operational processes that begin with the decision to buy a good or service and end with delivery and payment.
- *Audit and compliance*—supporting processes that focus on procurement performance measurement and reporting.

P2S often takes place in a project-based environment before the actual sourcing starts and thus affects internal business partners, therefore there are generally no real speed issues. However, S2C and P2P processes can be inordinately slow—especially in the eyes of business partners. The ramifications extend far beyond the

© Springer Nature Switzerland AG 2020

W. Schnellbächer, D. Weise, *Jumpstart to Digital Procurement*,
https://doi.org/10.1007/978-3-030-51984-1_6

procurement function. Companies that cannot respond fast enough to market changes lose a crucial source of competitive advantage. This holds just as true for the fashion retailer who needs to keep up with current trends and the automotive company that needs to source e-mobility quickly as it does for the airline that wants to have token items on hand to give away after the national team unexpectedly wins the world soccer championship.

To derive the greatest possible value from conventional methods, companies need to adopt a comprehensive approach along with three steps. First, they need to ground their speed optimization efforts in their strategic business objectives. Second, they need to delete steps where they are unnecessary. And third, they need to ensure a lean and uncomplicated setup.

Ground Optimization Efforts in Overall Business Objectives Strategic goals should guide all optimization efforts. Companies must first determine where speed is most needed and then balance those requirements with other considerations for optimal trade-offs. Equally the need for speed should be differentiated between categories. In an automotive company, for example, the sourcing strategy for a new battery technology should be finished earlier than the one for business travel. In any production-based company, the P2P process for critical parts should be set up in a speedy manner to avoid any production stops.

Delete Steps Where They Are Not Needed From strategy creation to checking the invoice before payment, any unnecessary step slows down the speed of procurement. Eliminating steps is therefore the number one way to accelerate the process— oftentimes, however, at the expense of other value dimensions (that is, savings, innovation, quality, sustainability, and risk). Usually a segmented approach is adopted because speed is more important in some categories than in others, so levers should be deployed accordingly. This segmented approach is referred to in the industry as channel strategy. For example, in categories considered critical to innovation, companies can reduce the number of selected suppliers to accelerate the speed of the S2C processes while keeping a larger pool of suppliers for categories in which savings are more important. This also holds true for P2P processes. While the requisition process for simple products such as office supplies should be straightforward, complex requisitions such as those for major capital projects require a lengthier process with multiple technical approvals. Developing a different channel for each type of requisition will help ensure that each process moves at the fastest pace possible (see Fig. 1). To enable a speedier requisition process for selected projects, the procurement function should allow bypassing selected time-consuming steps as a trade-off between speed and either savings or risk.

Ensure a Lean Setup Once process steps are reduced to the required minimum, it is important to ensure that remaining steps are conducted in the most efficient manner possible. In P2S and in S2C this is primarily a question of clear task splitting and the right training. It will help eliminate situations such as contract delays that occur when strategic buyers are forced to spend their time on tasks that should have been

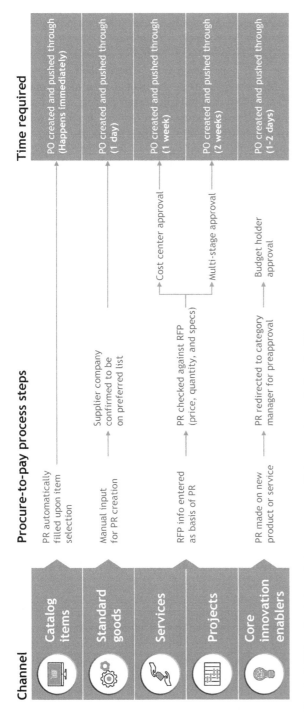

Fig. 1 A differentiated channel strategy ensures efficiency and organizational agility

allocated to operational buyers. In P2P however, a lot of time is wasted, for example, in following up on unclear or incomplete requisitions. A core pillar for a lean setup is therefore often a strong limitation of the number of employees allowed to make purchase requisitions. Limiting the number of such employees allows those who remain to gain more experience and, consequently, to perform their work with greater competence and speed. Moreover, fewer people would need to be trained in purchasing policies and systems, likely resulting in greater process compliance and lower resource usage. Stringent system setups represent another core pillar. Even conventional ERP systems should work in the channels introduced above and therefore in each category only ask for the information needed in the specific channel. Equally, ordering systems should not only rely on free text but have mandatory fields that ensure all crucial information points are delivered right before the purchasing request hits the procurement function and do not have to be collected afterwards by procurement employees.

Remaining Challenges

Although conventional approaches can accelerate procurement processes, there is still a lot of room for improvement. In operational process steps where a significant share of the buyer's workload is concentrated, compliance plays a key role and approval steps, for example, cannot be eliminated. Despite all the tailoring, training, and overall lean approaches in conventional best-in-class procurement functions, challenges remain—for instance, many of the tasks are manual and repetitive in nature. Digital tackles that using three levers.

- Speed up repetitive, time-consuming tasks, such as approvals or data transfers.
- Leverage machines in tasks requiring judgment and decisions.
- Automate even repetitive tasks that currently rely on human-to-human interaction such as phone calls.

How Digital Is Changing the Game: Robots as Our New Best Friends

Speed Up Repetitive, Time-Consuming Tasks, Such as Approvals or Data Transfers

Whenever a task can be completed using clear decision criteria and is clearly repetitive, it can be automated. Robotics replicate repetitive manual tasks at several times the speed and accuracy. They compare data, fill out forms, and, in the case of chatbots, even interact with users. For example, they can check the purchase requisitions from plants, translate the requisitions into purchase orders, and send these orders directly to business partners. After the orders are placed, bots check to see whether suppliers have responded and send reminders if necessary. Combined with optical character recognition, for example, robots can handle standard processes such as invoice checking or payment processing. The most common area of application for robotics are PR-PO processes. When a user submits a purchasing requisition (PR), different checks have to be conducted (user authority to buy in spend limit, category code,...) and then the request has to be transformed into a purchase order (PO) that the supplier can read. This process can largely be driven by a bot that can autonomously drive a large share of the validations and data transfers. The robot only contacts a buyer and asks for help if a specific information point is unclear or is missing. To date, a person has managed the process and employed a machine where helpful; now, it is a machine that drives the process and people are deployed to handle exceptions. Perceptively the systems within a company as well as to suppliers are to be harmonized in a manner that even robots only are needed in rare occasions because the data can be read-out right away.

> **How It Has Been Done: Robotics at a Construction Material Manufacturer**
>
> *A construction material manufacturer suspected that its suppliers were overcharging for materials and services. The company programmed a robot to automatically pull and compare all invoices, purchase orders, and data on goods received from the ERP system. Upon detecting a significant deviation, the bot took a screenshot and sent it to the responsible buyer, who then assessed the charge and followed up directly with the supplier. As a result of this automation-assisted effort, the manufacturer avoided extensive and time-consuming communication loops and reclaimed a total of €3.6 million from suppliers, 2% of its spend.*

Leverage Machines in Tasks Requiring Judgment and Decisions

A large number of procurement tasks require judgment and decisions, especially since data is frequently incomplete or wrong. In such cases, pure automation is equipped with machine learning algorithms that are able to recognize data patterns and propose decisions. These algorithms enable machines to learn and make choices based on their "intuition," that is, on the basis of past experience or a set of rules provided at the outset. Combining AI with bots can optimize many P2P processes.

Let us take the example of the PR-PO process again. Here, machine learning can significantly enhance classical robot processes or the direct connection of systems. While a bot can translate the requisition into a supplier-ready purchase order, it cannot detect errors; for example, it cannot tell whether the order has been waiting in the wrong purchase channel because a user filled out the wrong form. Machine learning can be trained to look for breaks in patterns that reveal an error, such as the wrong supplier name, a spend amount that is too small, or an address that is an office location rather than a plant site. It then asks the user to double-check the order. AI technologies can also decide whether it makes more sense to send a purchase order to a preferred supplier than to send a request for quotation (RfQ) to a few suppliers. Here, the technology analyzes not only the volume of the purchase but also certain characteristics of the category and the current state of the market. Ultimately, AI is useful for dealing with the results of an RfQ. Algorithms can evaluate suppliers according to different parameters (such as price, quality, and innovation potential) and identify the combination of supplier offers that creates the most value. This highly analytical, multi-round process evaluates tender results in a fraction of the time it would take humans. In addition, AI can automatically realize acceleration opportunities as the example below illustrates.

> **How It Has Been Done: AI-Based Tendering Evaluation Tool at a Packaging Producer**
>
> *A European packaging producer wanted to optimize the speed of its processes. Although robots were able to increase the speed of certain standard processes, supplier evaluations of greater complexity still took a long time. The company deployed an AI-based tendering evaluation tool to assess the results of a facility management RfQ that covered 162 sites, 6 subcategories, and a total of 85 suppliers. The tool analyzed the hundreds of possible supplier scenarios. At one extreme was the cherry-picking option that entailed 36 suppliers, each providing at least one service at the lowest price. This option would have resulted in the greatest savings but was neither desirable nor feasible because it involved too many suppliers. At the opposite extreme was the bundling option where just three suppliers would provide all of the items needed, but with significantly fewer savings for the packaging producer. The optimal solution was somewhere in the middle. The buyer and the manager saw that the tool accomplished in seconds what would have taken them 4 days—and after the 4 days they would not have been certain that they had found the best solution.*

Automate Even Repetitive Tasks That Currently Rely on Human-to-Human Interaction Such as Phone Calls

From AI-based solutions that assess situations and make decisions on the basis of their own "data-based intuition" it is a small step to personal interaction with internal business partners or even suppliers to reduce waiting time and increase speed. AI-based robots are either built as chatbots or voice over phone. These agents function in the same way as Apple's Siri, Google Home, or Amazon's Alexa. Accessing information from customers' ERP systems, the agents can serve as a hotline for internal employees and suppliers who have questions regarding the timing of deliveries. A typical application is that of a business partner following up an ongoing supplier delivery. He talks to a robot agent that searches the system for information on the order and translates the data entries found into a language understandable to the user on the phone. If the information found is not sufficient, the robot can also communicate to another robot that then sends a request to the supplier for further information or it can directly access the supplier system. Once it receives the information, it pro-actively calls the internal business partner again and provides the update.

Looking Ahead

In the future, the speed and efficiency of procurement processes will become even more vital to competitive advantage. Companies that accelerate their processes now will find themselves ahead of the game later on. However, process digitization is a major undertaking, requiring vast amounts of time and resources. CPOs need to lead the charge in determining which processes to focus on and which technologies to deploy. Their vision is crucial to realizing the full potential of digital.

Enablers That Make It Work

Enablers to foster speed are clear, lean, and easily understandable *processes*. Optimized processes promote speed because they establish efficient and agile ways of responding to change and remove ambiguity regarding how things should be done. With streamlined and digitized S2C processes, procurement can react faster towards market price increases and re-negotiate contracts even before their impact the cost base, for example. A second enabler is the *people* both inside and outside the procurement function. As procurement systems have become more sophisticated, the purchasing experience has come to resemble the online shopping experience, which is fairly intuitive. But there may still be occasions when employees need to purchase items or services that aren't featured in the catalog. Without proper training in the more complex procedures required in such situations, they are likely to make orders via phone or email, slowing down the process. A training program that covers both online and in-person procedures is a good way to quickly familiarize people with the purchasing process while promoting a high rate of adoption and raising awareness of the importance of adhering to established P2P processes. The third enabler lies in *performance management*. Monitoring the pace of activity along the entire chain of S2C and P2P processes is essential for the categories that are strategically most important. Dashboards can be used to communicate findings to procurement management and key external stakeholders. It is also critical to monitor employee compliance. Although circumventing systems and processes may seem like a faster way of getting something done, it can greatly compromise speed. Establishing KPIs with a clear focus on speed makes it possible to keep track of individual employees on a regular basis.

Risk: Predicting the Future and Acting on It

The world is becoming increasingly interconnected, which creates complex interdependencies in global supply chains. At the same time, uncertainty is growing, with companies being exposed to a wide range of risks threatening their business. Chinese factory closures due to natural disasters or labor strikes in South Africa plant cause standstills in Germany and trade barriers increase sourcing costs. The consequences are significant: The insurance company AON estimates noninsured costs of $134 billion from natural disasters in one year alone.

CPOs must excel in managing the risk associated with the supply base. They must be able to keep the supply chain running with all goods and services required at the right quality, sustainability, and time. In the past, procurement employees and subject matter experts discussed risks intensively based on their instincts and past events. This cumbersome approach produced false results, as identified by Nobel Prize winner Daniel Kahneman in the "representativeness heuristic": We overestimate the likelihood of recent events and have a distorted view, which in turn disproportionately exposes us to new events. Leading companies overcome this overexposure through a holistic approach that assesses risks correctly, selects optimal mitigation levers, equips risk management with digital, and chooses best-suited enablers.

Starting Position: Building a Solid Understanding of What Might Happen

Risk management today is strongly characterized by *identifying and evaluating potential risks*. We need to differentiate between two risk types: black swans and detectable risks. A black swan is an outlier beyond regular expectations as no data from the past can credibly point to its likelihood. This includes rare natural disasters and unexpected political movements, such as sudden barriers after decades of free trade. It is common to rationalize events as predictable in hindsight, with the risk assessment program being assigned the blame for failing to predict their occurrence.

© Springer Nature Switzerland AG 2020
W. Schnellbächer, D. Weise, *Jumpstart to Digital Procurement*,
https://doi.org/10.1007/978-3-030-51984-1_7

At the opposite end of the spectrum is the detectable risk for which the likelihood of occurrence is determined by observing previous occurrences. To predict such risks, easy-to-recognize signals are used initially, such as a supplier's deteriorating financial performance. The sophistication of detection increases by adding more signals, such as weather forecasts to predict water shortages.

In clearly segmenting these two risk types, leading companies assess the impact and thus the consequences of risks by simulating profit and reputational losses, such as missed deliveries or damaged assets. This is done, for example, by linking a bill-of-materials to final SKUs in the ERP system to simulate supply disruptions of components or suppliers. The difference between the two risk types becomes apparent in Fig. 1, which depicts a framework commonly used in risk management.

Events marked as *high risk* have a large impact on the business and close monitoring is set up to ensure fast responses. *Operational risk* is a minor disturbance that occurs frequently and causes smaller disruptions; for example, late shipments or customs issues. It is easy to overlook this as nonexistential, although it presents an impact opportunity by optimizing mitigation using breakdown frequency as a parameter. To manage *disruptive risk*, leading procurement organizations leverage sensitivity analyses to decide on an acceptable risk exposure, such as identifying particularly harmful SKUs in case of disruptions or assessing geographical supplier distributions to determine vulnerable regions. Casually monitoring the development of the *limited risk* category provides early warning signs of changes to the risk type and impact. This includes continuously screening for increasing occurrences of risks that may eventually become detectable risks.

An often underestimated factor in understanding risk is the aspired depth of reporting. Procurement professionals should neither get lost in the details nor stay at too high a level to make the right assumptions. Multiple layers of transparency have to be set up based on a clear segmentation into owners of different risks. The CPO reports overall procurement risk to executive management and needs access to category overviews. Category managers need their overall category risk and drill-downs to the supplier and SKU levels. Visualizing risk in real time is crucial to translating data into useable information.

After seeing their risks clearly, procurement professionals need to *choose and apply the right risk management levers*. The *transparency* lever thoroughly evaluates risk buckets to improve the assessment; for example, by auditing supplier factories to assess disruption threats resulted from for example insufficient production safety standards. The *preventive mitigation* lever minimizes risks before they impair performance. For example, the "buffer inventory" tool is effective due to its quantifiable mitigation impact, allowing for optimization based on risk assessment. "Dual sourcing" is a powerful tool for reducing single supplier risk, but understanding the supply chain's geographical setup and company interlinkages is crucial. The *reactive mitigation* lever reduces the damage caused by materialized risks. It requires a quick selection of the right levers and engagement of the organizational owners to make swift decisions. Simulations test emergency procedures, such as supplier approval speed to reestablish supply from alternative sources or the use of operations task force experts ready to be deployed at supplier sites to reestablish supply.

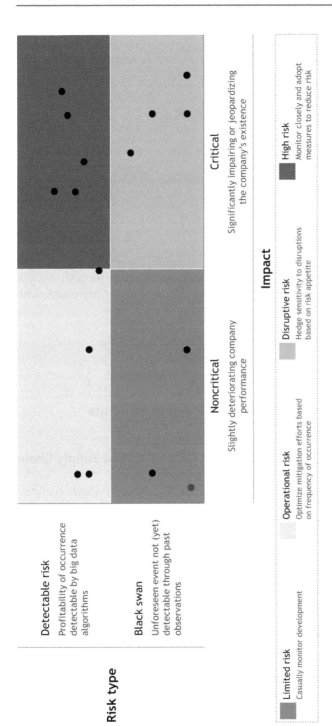

Fig. 1 Risk assessment framework

Fig. 2 Illustrative selection of risk management levers

Figure 2 shows an illustrative selection of risk management levers segmenting them into these three structural elements.

Remaining Challenges

Like the other value dimensions, the conventional best-in-class methods for risk leave challenges that can be additionally addressed by new digital approaches with two pillars:

- Establishing transparency throughout the end-to-end supply chain.
- Ensuring the right risks are tackled with the right lever set.

How Digital Is Changing the Game: Bringing Structure to Black Swans

Establishing Transparency Throughout the End-to-End Supply Chain

In the business world with complex supply chain routing through multiple countries and regions, it's not sufficient to focus on tier-1 suppliers only. Global companies have to establish and maintain a constant visibility along the entire supply chain, extending from direct suppliers to raw materials providers. Establishing such thorough transparency involves ongoing extraction and processing of gigantic volumes of data, something that is not feasible with conventional risk management. Digitization and technology development opens up new opportunities for procurement to tackle this challenge.

The key is to build on a comprehensive repository of big data as the basis for risk management. Starting with internal sources, such as supplier performance metrics for on-time deliveries or defective parts per millions (PPMs), allows deteriorating performance to be detected early on so that timely corrective action can be taken. Simple external data sources improve risk detection, such as monitoring a supplier's credit rating. But all of this can only detect risks that are based on the supplier setup itself and does not take into account the larger political or environmental trends that equally pose danger to a company. To address such risks, the location, time, and content of tweets on the social media platform Twitter can be tracked to detect political uprisings at an accelerated speed, for example, to predict national political instability or send an early warning about strike action that might impair delivery. The assessment of these macro trends based on millions of publically available data points can easily be outsourced to specialized vendors with tailored search engines and algorithms to monitor selected supply markets. Supplier-level risk assessment is also improving; for instance, through joint platforms to rate suppliers and by actively monitoring government watch lists to detect sanctioned suppliers.

Risk visualizations are automatic and link data sources in an interactive dashboard, readily available to users in real time; for example, using tools such as Tableau or PowerBI that enable users to visualize the overall risk and take a closer look at desired segments of whole supply chain.

How It Has Been Done: Global Supply Chain Monitoring at a Leading Manufacturer in the Optical Industry

A leading optical systems manufacturer has faced a complex, globally connected supply chain extending from Southeast Asia through North America to Europe. Due to limited visibility across the upstream supply chain beyond tier-1 suppliers and extremely high capacity utilization at suppliers' sites, any risk issues could lead to supply disruption and cause negative financial impact. To tackle the challenge, the company worked with various data and software providers and introduced an integrated supply chain risk management (SCRM) system. By linking the SCRM system to the company's ERP system and external data sources, all relevant data were automatically extracted and populated on a platform in order to facilitate permanent supply chain monitoring. Screening thousands of social media and online sources enabled timely identification of risk signals and delivery of early warnings to business stakeholders. This greatly shortened the reaction time and minimized the impact on production and delivery. A plant fire at a subcontracted supplier, for example, triggered a warning signal that was sent to the procurement team only a couple of minutes after the fire was reported.

Ensuring the Right Risks Are Tackled with the Right Lever Set

Agile supply risk management does not stop at establishing deep visibility across the supply chain. It goes without saying that combining large data sources and interpreting that huge volume of data means an enormous, resource-heavy task for companies. Robotic process automation (RPA) considerably reduces the effort of mapping and following up on risks, which is the major operational hurdle in risk management today. For example, RPA scrapes internal data such as invoices and external data from social media platforms and stores it in a combined warehouse. It also assesses risks by seamlessly linking bill-of-materials and sales data in the ERP system.

AI adds a good measure of sophistication to the detection and interpretation of risk signals by using big data to consolidate and analyze data sources. An algorithm could be run on a company's suppliers by combining the macroeconomic risks of political instability and natural disasters with supplier-specific risks, such as delivery performance and credit ratings. By leveraging machine learning, AI constantly improves its algorithms by observing which events led to disruptions and which did not, thereby adjusting its risk assessments. Detecting black swans still remains a challenge but a challenge that can be handled. While humans purely relied on their intuition and memory of a few data points, the AI-based systems can weigh up information from millions of data points and across countries and industries to calculate possible scenarios. This enables earlier risk detection and it especially widens the scope—typically from pure financial risks to geopolitical and technological risk types based on big masses of data. Based on its assessment, AI uses the risk management levers to propose faster and more precise mitigation actions. As an example, it adjusts buffer inventory to equilibrium based on its knowledge of expected disruption times and inventory costs. Machine learning makes it increasingly easy to choose the right levers, as it observes their outcomes given disruptive events and makes improvements as it goes along. For instance, when attempting to identify the risk of a supplier's bankruptcy, big data can provide the balance sheet and reveal when the supplier sends invoices, or even monitor the supplier's input cost to assess its profit margin over time and use that information to foresee bankruptcy. The power of AI comes in to weigh up all of these input parameters and constantly calculate probabilities. Below is an example of how real-time risk management becomes possible in the technology industry based on AI and big data.

How It Has Been Done: Leveraging Cognitive Technology in Supply Risk Management at a Multinational Technology Corporation

Under constant pressure to maintain smooth and reliable delivery with its global supply chain, a leading technology corporation implemented a Transparent Supply Chain Initiative consisting of three major pillars. Besides end-to-end supply chain visibility and availability of real-time data, the company also applied cognitive technology and advanced analytics to facilitate quicker issue response. Utilization of these technology possibilities prevented the team from being overwhelmed by extensive information flows around different types of issues and provided actionable recommendations to focus the team on making decisions and triggering measures. Moreover, the cognitive technology continuously learned from the successes and failures of previous events to generate better results in future planning and responses. Empowered by this dynamic, digitalized risk management "playbook," the company's response to supply chain disruption shortened from 18–21 days to just hours, and more than $40 million was saved as a result of optimized inventory level and freight costs.

Looking Ahead

The challenges in managing supplier risks will continue to grow. Even more so than today, procurement organizations will need to place a strong emphasis on comprehensive risk management. Buyers will have to get used to systems that advise them on what to focus on and which levers to apply to reduce their specific risk exposure. Many tools are already available in an easily sourceable manner, others can be built in individual solutions, leveraging artificial intelligence in particular. Companies that make the right investments now will have a significant advantage over their competitors in the future. Not only will they have refined and tailored their own tool solutions, even more importantly, but they will also have selected the right data fields and started collecting the required data internally and from suppliers. Without that data, digital risk management will not work.

> **Enablers that Make It Work**
>
> Procurement professionals will not have their risks under control if they have not embedded enablement properly in their operating model. All enabler dimensions are crucial for solid risk management; for instance, in *organization*, ensuring that risk management is part of the category buyer's role descriptions, or in *processes*, that there are risk-limiting activities in critical categories, such as regular supplier audits as part of the sourcing process. *Collaboration* between suppliers, procurement, and internal business partners builds transparency regarding which risks should be focused on throughout the supply chain.
>
> Particular emphasis, however, needs to be placed on the dimensions of *people* and *performance management*. It is crucial to educate employees in the organization in how to perceive and manage risk, and to provide guidance for tailoring both risk assessments and mitigation to category contexts. Enabling buyers to leverage the digital solutions described is also essential to bringing risk management firmly under control. With category managers measured against other KPIs, performance management must include risk measures to incentivize adequate prioritization of the topic, such as by measuring the prospective efforts of preventive levers or the value saved by reactive efforts.

Part II

Enablers: What Makes It Work

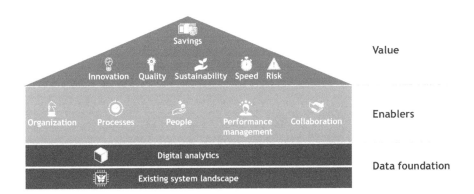

Value

Enablers

Data foundation

Organization: Building the Procurement Function of the Future

The first part of this book provided an extensive overview of the value that procurement brings to companies—having advanced from a function purely focusing on savings to a strategic partner also securing access to critical innovations, supplier quality, assurance of sustainability, delivery speed, and a limited risk exposure.

We now take a deeper look at the enablers that make the procurement function work, starting with the *organization* that ensures new digital tools and applications are sufficiently leveraged. To achieve this, CPOs need to think holistically. Every role must be challenged and changed if necessary, from those of strategic buyers to those of purchasing controllers. Some, such as robotic maintenance engineers, will emerge while others, such as operational and transactional buyers, will largely disappear. Leading companies that actively transform their procurement organizations will gain a large strategic advantage over their peers in terms of much more powerful value generation.

Starting Position: Deploying Resources Where Value Is Created

When reviewing their organizational design, CPOs strive for excellence throughout the entire procurement process. Strategic buyers define how a category must be sourced and they perform tasks that span all planning-to-strategy (P2S) and source-to-contract (S2C) processes. Equally, an optimal procurement organization takes into account the geographic location of both business partners and suppliers. The objective of strategic procurement is to fulfill business requirements while maximizing the value delivered from the supply base. Operational procurement provides support and drives the procure-to-pay (P2P) processes. In addition, process design often provides support for procurement control and research. To gain a holistic view, CPOs should segment their teams into three groups when defining a best-in-class procurement organization: Strategic buyers, operational/tactical buyers,

© Springer Nature Switzerland AG 2020
W. Schnellbächer, D. Weise, *Jumpstart to Digital Procurement*,
https://doi.org/10.1007/978-3-030-51984-1_8

support teams. In addition they should keep three more excellence dimensions in mind: role definitions, cross-functional interfaces, and total sizing.

Strategic Buyers The objective of strategic procurement is to satisfy business requirements while maximizing the value delivered from the supply base. Two core tasks are inherent in the organizational setup. The first is to find the right number of strategic buyers. Typically, a third of the employees in the procurement function are dedicated to strategic tasks. Second, these strategic resources must be allocated to the categories in which they can create the highest value—in most companies this means the highest savings success. In advanced procurement organizations, the understanding of value creation goes beyond savings and includes the dimensions of innovation, quality, sustainability, speed, and risk, each with its own unique requirements.

Operational/Transactional Buyers The team of operational buyers must be set up with a strong focus on efficiency. Their activities include operational tasks, such as smaller negotiations and supplier follow-ups, as well as transactional and repetitive activities, such as processing PRs to POs. Operational/transactional teams represent by far the largest group within the procurement function. Not only must they be correct in size, they should also be well integrated into the team of strategic buyers; operational tasks often closely follow strategic activities. Conversely, transactional tasks have a strong potential for economies of scale and are therefore organized using different steps in the value chain, such as invoice checking. CPOs place particular emphasis on efficiency here as operational and transactional teams make up two-thirds of the procurement workforce. Therefore, transactional activities in particular are often outsourced or offshored in shared service centers to ensure the greatest economies of scale as well as to leverage labor arbitrage.

Support Teams Procurement support functions typically consist of purchasing controlling, process excellence, and research teams, and the teams are usually smaller than those of strategic and operational buyers. Purchasing controlling is responsible for financial as well as operational data—especially in the field of savings generation. A best-in-class setup makes the category-independent controlling team the only credible authority for any savings approval and, thus, the only instance capable of validating the savings successes of buying teams. The process excellence group not only defines and continuously improves working procedures—strategic and operational in nature—it is also typically responsible for the existing system landscape. Last, research teams are specialized in finding information for category teams, be it about suppliers in LCC countries, market trends in commodities, or the overall risk in supply chain markets. Each support function needs to be well integrated into category teams, representing a core task for CPOs.

Role Definitions Although roles in procurement are currently not all that diverse, many companies struggle to find the right distribution within their teams. Strategic buyers in particular are often not given sufficient time to drive forward significant value levers because they are continuously being dragged into operational issues, such as following up on undelivered stock, coordinating deliveries with small suppliers, or even clarifying unclear orders. Leading organizations implement a clear division of roles as reflected in the well-known RASCI matrices. Each role is obliged to focus on the assigned delivery fields, ensuring that sufficient time and responsibility is dedicated to them.

Cross-Functional Interfaces In leading organizations, cross-functional collaboration is orchestrated through tandem teams of buyers and core business partners. Tandem targets for these teams ensure collaboration toward a uniting goal. This mechanism promotes procurement to a strategic partner; it acts as a peer. A new organizational structure is required to reflect this proximity to business partners. One model used by leading procurement organizations is to introduce dedicated key account management (KAM). To establish effective, powerful procurement key account management, it is essential that it mirrors the business partner's setup and agrees on common targets, cascaded down in both parts of the organization; otherwise a sense of connection is lost as a result of friction in day-to-day operations.

Total Sizing The best split between operational and strategic procurement has been defined above. The total sizing defines the ideal number of FTEs for the procurement organization as a whole. The objective is to have a spend range that strikes the ideal balance of being low enough for the buyer to achieve strong results, but still high enough to justify salary and total cost. Typically, the managed spend per buyer is a common indicator. For indirect procurement, CPOs should aim for a managed spend of €22–25 million per FTE. When distributing the resulting FTEs across functions, a relatively even distribution between strategic procurement and operational/support teams has proven best.

Upcoming Challenges

In the future, CPOs must think critically about the changes that digitization brings to procurement and actively steer them into their organization. Each team member in each of the three groups introduced will be subject to significant change. Equally, the three further excellence dimensions (role definitions, cross-functional interfaces, total sizing) need to be properly thought through.

How Digital Is Changing the Game: A New Type of Buyer Pool

In pre-thinking the upcoming changes, CPOs must equally balance an increased demand for value creation with a strong push for higher procurement efficiency. This includes, among other things, delegating buyers to categories in which the highest value can be created; preparing operational buyers, suppliers, and internal business partners to work with robotics on everyday tasks; creating new roles and role requirements dedicated to leveraging the full potential of digital; and adjusting the total sizing accordingly. Thus, after prioritizing strategic value, the design phase of what constitutes best practice for a digital procurement organization begins, tackling each of the six dimensions of excellence.

Strategic Buyers Digitization boosts the significance of strategic procurement, since value can be delivered in areas not even considered in pre-digital times. We have seen a high number of examples in the first part of this book tackling the full bandwidth of value generation from savings, innovation, quality, sustainability, speed, and preventing risks. The following is a list of but a few highlights:

- AI negotiation coaches increase *savings* by telling buyers which approach to use in each situation, leading to significantly increased cost-reduction effects.
- AI helps identify which supplier has the highest *innovation* potential and how to incentivize it best.
- AI-based mechanisms improve *quality*, as they can predict the category group and supplier with which the next incident is likely to occur.
- Blockchain helps establish trust and safeguard *sustainability* in several links in the supply chain.
- Robotics makes procurement three to five times faster, increasing *speed* in even conservative and very risk-averse scenarios.
- Cognitive intelligence helps foresee and prevent *risk* in complex global supply chains.

Consequently, based on these new possibilities, strategic buyers will have to be relocated among categories in which the highest value can be generated. This value constantly changes with the digital possibilities but equally so with the specific company strategy. In the automotive industry, for example, the sourcing of new technologies has become a core task in the trend for fast-moving portfolios of car components such as e-mobility, UI, or UX. Strategic buyers are delegated to categories with a small spend but high innovative potential, leveraging big data and other solutions to find the most promising suppliers—even among smaller start-ups. Furthermore, analytical tools can reveal new savings opportunities, as we have seen in the first section of this book, making necessary a re-allocation based purely on savings. The simple allocation of buyers to categories by spend is over. Every CPO must frequently review where this must be done, taking advantage of new tools and solutions to ensure that the highest value can be generated for their company—and that their strategic buyers are allocated accordingly.

Operational/Transactional Buyers When digitizing procurement, automation is our new best friend for operational and transactional activities, as these usually include repetitive, manual tasks. They can either be taken care of by means of simple robotic solutions, such as invoice checking, or they can be replaced by robots working in conjunction with AI whereby the latter works alongside the robot; for instance, to determine whether an order is being placed in the right category based on heuristic algorithms. Overall, the operational buying staff can be reduced by a minimum of 50% relative to current levels. CPOs must take this into account when planning and hiring their operational and transactional teams. In addition, they must prepare all stakeholders within and outside the procurement function to learn to interact with automated machines in day-to-day life. This new skill has to become part of the buyer's job profiles—especially in operational and transactional teams. The buyers will have to reply to requests issued by machines, accept answers to their questions from machines, and reactivate robotics processes that might be stuck because a piece of information is missing. CPOs must not only drive the transition to automation by introducing robotics and finding new tasks for the resources that are freed up, they must also prepare the remaining operational buyers, suppliers, and internal business partners to work with robotics in everyday tasks.

Support Teams Support teams are growing significantly in importance in these digital times and CPOs need to pro-actively manage this increasing relevance. Leading procurement functions are growing the size of these teams by about 100%, with employees who will be working in new roles dedicated to helping the entire function exploit the digital potential. A few examples: Master data teams ensure all relevant information is not only collected but also stored centrally so that it is accessible for core analytics. These teams define and monitor data collection processes and, if necessary, new ways of working to ensure that all necessary information is stored. In addition, they also define "sources of truth" in clarifying what information is correct should there be several contradicting data points. AI programmers, as another example, help buyers arrive at the right conclusions from the existing data. They need to be as close to data analytics procedures as they are to procurement tools and tasks. Programmers of AI negotiation coaches, for example, need to be familiar with the different negotiation approaches, including their strengths and weaknesses. The robotic maintenance engineer is another new role—these employees program and maintain the bots used in operational process steps. They need to be equally knowledgeable in the technical aspects of their systems as well as the requirements in the operational processes to which they introduce the robots (e.g., compliance). While the existing enabling functions will maintain both their importance and size, these new roles will have to be added and CPOs must be actively on the lookout for qualified employees able to fulfill these tasks. In addition, in larger procurement organizations, a digital change agent should be installed temporarily to head the digital changes.

Role Definitions In pre-digital times, CPOs had to ensure that strategic and operational buyers were clearly distinguished in terms of the description and execution of their roles. Now that a variety of new roles has been introduced, this task becomes even more challenging. In addition, the existing role portfolio is also experiencing a shift in the required skillset, with operational buyers being required to handle RPA and strategic buyers being required to leverage big data, digital analytics, and AI. To make matters more complex still, the shift is not equal between categories. Just as value generation changes in different categories, so too do the required skill sets for buyers. IT buyers need to be able to handle AI to stay on top of innovation potential; MRO buyers need to leverage it for quality control. Office supplies, on the other hand, need catalog solutions and RPA, while consulting might not require any profile change. It is therefore important for procurement to determine only the profiles currently required throughout the specific categories and functions while also anticipating future needs and reflecting them accordingly in the portfolio. CPOs will have to proactively manage the increased complexity in more diverse and, at the same time, more agile role descriptions. The new profiles, such as AI programmers, need to be included and clearly differentiated in their tasks from other digital (such as master data teams) and conventional roles (such as the strategic buyers working with the AI algorithms). At the same time, role descriptions need to be kept agile to ensure they can be adapted intelligently in response to new technologies, such as new robotics taking over tasks in operational purchasing or AI mechanisms opening new value creation fields in strategic procurement.

Cross-Functional Interfaces Through digitization, the value delivery of procurement expands and interfaces become more dynamic. More than ever before, digitization enables procurement to upgrade its role from that of a transactional service provider to one of a strategic business partner on an equal footing. For IT, for example, procurement can help spot innovations, while manufacturing will benefit from procurement's prediction of supplier-related quality failures. Interfaces are therefore broadening in scope, which requires procurement to understand the right value drivers for each business partner, the most powerful digital advantage, and the resulting organizational anchoring. As digitization expands, CPOs must ensure that a strong focus is placed on a thorough understanding of the value that business partners really expect from procurement. They must actively promote this value added and, based on the interfaces, define increased room for procurement to act. It is no longer a simple provider of savings but of innovation, quality, secured sustainability, speed, and reduced risk.

Total Sizing As we have seen, digitization strongly affects all parts of the procurement organization, from strategic category managers and operational buyers to support teams. While in the strategic categories we can expect to see buyers moving primarily between categories based on new opportunities for added value, in operational procurement we will see an average 50% drop and in the support team an average 100% increase. Naturally, the ideal size needs to be determined by each CPO individually on the basis of the impact of digitization on value generation opportunities as well as increased efficiencies. Overall, however, the total size of procurement organizations will decrease—primarily due to automation in operational procurement and AI in tactical procurement. The reduction potential will amount to around 30%. CPOs need to ensure that the right positions are built up to drive their function toward the future. Simultaneously, they need to ensure that the HR budget of operational and transactional buyers is freed up in a socially sustainable yet effective manner.

Figure 1 combines all the described changes into one comprehensive overview.

How It Has Been Done: Digitized Procurement at an Automotive OEM

A leading automotive OEM recently implemented changes in its procurement organization in an effort to realize savings, improve quality, and prevent risks. To achieve these results, the company needed to transform procurement along with three core factors. First, direct reporting to the CPO was established for support teams. Second, strategic buyers were shifted to categories in which the highest value was expected to be created over the next few years. Those categories with lower strategic potential, such as stampings or tubes, significantly "lost" buyers while newer categories, such as UI/UX, were equipped with proportionally high levels of resources compared to their spend. Third, new role profiles were defined—particularly in the support teams—to sufficiently manage procurement data, specialize in detailed analyses, and develop advanced analytics tools going forward. In one role three robotics maintenance engineers had to be hired from the market since these capabilities were not present in the existing setup despite five bots already running in the function. These specialists were set the target of increasing the bots to 15 within one year. Another new dedicated role was master data, which was given the task of preparing the ground for future AI analytics.

Looking Ahead

Digitization puts procurement at the crossroads of success and failure. One of the most crucial factors that determine which road a procurement function will take is its ability to unlock and anchor the opportunities provided by digitization within its organizational setup. This cannot be done without rethinking the organizational structure in the digital context. Procurement has long fought to earn a seat at the table. Establishing a digital organization will not only ensure it keeps that seat but also increase its influence.

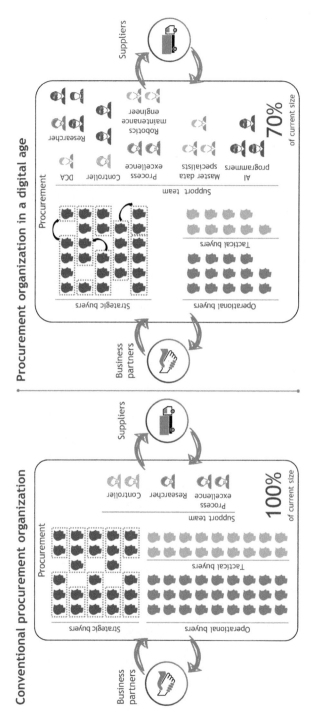

Fig. 1 Organizational changes from a conventional to a digitized procurement function

Processes: Clear, Lean, and Automated

Processes define the work within a function and at its interfaces. They are the guiding grid along which work procedures take place, making them pivotal to any value generation. Consequently, process efficiency and effectiveness strongly benefit from the digital revolution. And even more so, getting processes right significantly determines the overall success of digital applications within the function.

Starting Position: Ensuring a Lean Setup

The section on "speed" introduced three main categories of procurement activities. Planning-to-strategy (P2S) covers strategic processes starting with the planning of the entire procurement function and ending with category strategy definitions. Source-to-contract (S2C) describes operational processes from defining sourcing projects to the signing of supplier contracts. And lastly, procure-to-pay (P2P), which contains operational processes from the decision to buy a good or service to delivery and payment. To ensure an effective and efficient setup, leading CPOs to orient their processes on the overall company as well as the procurement strategy; set up comprehensive process descriptions; and separate value-adding procedures from different stakeholders. As with any enabler, the process landscape needs to be *derived from the overall company strategy* and developed into a procurement strategy that includes the optimal setup of processes in each one of these three activity types. BCG's Procurement House provides this framework. If *quality* is crucial, processes need to contain rigorous technical checks. If *sustainability* compliance, for example, is key, then the checks should focus on the reliability of suppliers to keep promises of environmental protection. If *speed*, however, plays a crucial role, the checks are to be limited. Since the strategic importance and also the relevance of value dimensions along BCG's Procurement House vary by category, the process setup will also need to be tailored. In the P2S, this can mean that in a category that is *innovation*-focused, searching for suppliers takes a great deal of time to ensure finding the best-suited partners. In a category where *quality* matters most,

© Springer Nature Switzerland AG 2020

W. Schnellbächer, D. Weise, *Jumpstart to Digital Procurement*,
https://doi.org/10.1007/978-3-030-51984-1_9

the requirements for a supplier to be accepted in the strategy are set quite high. P2P categories focused on *speed* set relatively high approval limits, so many orders can be taken without time-consuming cross-checks. On the other hand, categories focusing on *savings* have low approval levels, so small orders also need to go through procurement.

It is crucial that these setups are reflected in *comprehensive process descriptions*. While in P2S these descriptions leave a lot of room for creativity and individual tailoring to specific situations, in P2P they become much more thorough, detailed, and concrete process steps along with four layers. The upper layer simply provides a high-level process view and the lowest level contains very detailed working steps for each employee, such as in the approval of requisitions. It is key that the process description leads to global standardization to ensure that the best-in-class procedure is integrated throughout all units of a company. It is equally important that the operational descriptions are not only distributed and implemented in procurement but are also used where they matter most. Outside of the procurement function, they are translated into buying guides that inform users how to order certain goods and services commensurate with the process requirements along with the company's value ambition for procurement. A typical example of buying guide descriptions is a listing of the minimum information requirements needed in a purchase requisition before it goes to procurement to be translated into a purchasing order. Another example of a buying guide rule is the "No PO—No Payment" setup which is clearly communicated to internal business partners.

Beyond that, the process descriptions need to be written in such a way as to separate the value-adding procedures of different stakeholders. This is crucial within the procurement function where strategic and operational process steps need to be clearly split. If such a split is not properly embedded in the processes, the strategic employees are oftentimes overburdened with operational tasks, leading to a limited focus on the value-adding activities; clear role splits along processes prevent that. Additionally, separation along the processes is crucial for outsourced or offshored units. Outsourcing and offshoring typically take place in P2P procedures at the end of procurement's value chain or in nonstrategic categories. Since face-to-face contact with the outsourced or offshored units is rare, it needs to be clear what working steps they will take and what is to be done by the core procurement team. Hub and spoke systems play a crucial role here. The spoke system liaises with operations and helps business partners hands-on with any supply issues, mostly through remaining buyers in the plants. The hub system is where the remote offshored and/or outsourced unit places orders, resolves exceptions, or follows up with POs. Last, the descriptions regulate the interfaces between procurement and internal business partners as well as between procurement and suppliers. Here it is particularly important to establish a set of rules stating that commercial discussions and discussions with commercial consequences need the involvement of procurement and are ideally led by procurement right from the outset.

Upcoming Challenges

In digital times, CPOs must ask themselves whether their function's processes support the digital rollout or whether some process requirements actually hinder it. Overall, two upcoming challenges stand out.

- Setting up processes to allow the automation of redundant work steps
- Ensuring processes capture data sufficiently for AI-based steering

How Digital Is Changing the Game: Doubling Down on Clarity and the Capture of Data

Setting Up Processes to Allow the Automation of Redundant Work Steps

Robotics will take over at least 50% of the operational processes and a significant share of strategic procedures. This can only happen if processes are written down and implemented in a detailed manner according to the four-layer descriptions laid out above. Each work step needs to be clearly described, including core responsibilities and timing. This not only makes it easier to program bots but more importantly, it ensures robotics and humans can collaborate smoothly later on. It eases the processes of defining what the robot will do and what it will not do.

> **How It Has Been Done: Automation of Operational Buying Function**
> *A leading automotive OEM recently automated the operational buying function of its indirect procurement. While it only took 3 weeks to program the bots, prior to that 10 weeks of effort were necessary to detail the process descriptions from the granular level that is needed for any programming. As a result, 20% of the tasks of operational buyers were automated and the buyers had more time for more strategic value-creating efforts. In particular, the threshold from which awards were renegotiated over the phone was reduced from €50,000 to €5000 in volume, leading to more than 8000 additional negotiations and savings of €12 million.*

Ensuring Processes Capture Data Sufficiently for AI-based Steering

When looking at the major role artificial intelligence will play in procurement's value generation—from savings to innovation, quality, sustainability compliance, speed, and risk avoidance—the vast amount of data needed becomes obvious. Artificial intelligence relies heavily on the right data sets in order to propose the best choices. A function's process landscape plays a crucial role here. It first determines, through its process step descriptions, what data points are generated. The sourcing requirements set in category strategies, for example, define which analytics or negotiation tools should be used. These tools centrally determine data needs and are therefore crucial to what data is generated. Another example is the usage of the AI negotiation coach (see the "Savings" section). If process descriptions make usage of AI negotiation coaches mandatory, a lot of data on the sourcing situation has to be entered first. Then processes define what generated data will be stored. These requirements are especially essential in operational procurement where the storing of technical and commercial information for each order should be compulsory. Moreover, the processes define *where* the data is stored. IT data flows need to ensure there is only one source of truth in a central system. The central system can be connected to different data storage media but only if any data updates run synchronically.

How It Has Been Done: Setting Up the Tail Spend of the Operational Buying Function
When a European chemical producer set up its tail spend management, 10,000 line items had to be managed. After extensive data collection from fragmented sources throughout the company and a large-scale tail spend tender with 6% savings, the core challenge was to keep the data transparency, and with it the savings successes sustainable. A separate unit of seven FTEs was founded which quickly identified the sourcing processes as key to keeping information up to date, including the ability to keep prices down. So, strict requirements were put in place in which data either had to be generated or approved for each order, not only in the commercial but also in the technical dimension. These data points included a new chemical clustering exclusively set up for the tail spend, whether distributors were part of the supply chain or whether the specification included religious requirements such as halal or kosher.

Looking Ahead

Going forward, CPOs need to thoroughly review their processes, not only in terms of whether they are lean and support procurement's aspired value dimensions, but also whether they are set up in a way that supports transformation to a digital function. It will be particularly imperative to review processes, questioning how they support data generation for upcoming AI solutions. This may call for new requirements specifying what data has to be stored and resistance is likely due to the burden of additional data work. CPOs need to ensure that the new processes are still meticulously followed as the basis for future data-based steering.

People: A New Skill Set for New Roles

People is without a doubt the most crucial enabler dimension in BCG's Procurement House. When managers fail to manage their people well, they can excel in everything else but they will not succeed. However, at the same time, the people dimension is by far the most complex one to tackle and, therefore, also requires the highest degree of attention from CPOs and managers alike. Typically, when successfully implementing new tools, only 10% depends on the right selection and 20% on the available data, whereas 70% depends on the extent to which people adapt to the inherent changes.

Starting Position: Driving Both the Skill and Will of Employees

Best-in-class people management encompasses two dimensions: the employees' *ability* to perform in terms of their skill set and their *willingness* to perform with regard to their motivation. The *skill/will* matrix is derived from the model of situational leadership developed by Paul Hersey and Ken Blanchard. It guides leading CPOs in their people management and divides employees into four clusters: procurement superstars as a leading group to be empowered; up-and-comers should receive strong training based on their high level of willingness to perform; experts with less willingness but strong skills are to be motivated either with financial incentives, recognition, or ideally their intrinsic attitude; and last of all, there are candidates with neither the skill nor the will to be phased out (see Fig. 1).

Ability to Perform

In best-in-class companies, requirements for strategic buyers include a wide variety of tasks, some of them analytical and some interpersonal in nature, while others primarily require rigidity, such as data management (see Fig. 2). The variety of tasks is so wide that only few buyers excel in all dimensions. In addition, strategic tasks

© Springer Nature Switzerland AG 2020
W. Schnellbächer, D. Weise, *Jumpstart to Digital Procurement*,
https://doi.org/10.1007/978-3-030-51984-1_10

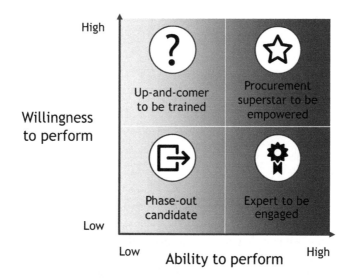

Fig. 1 Employees' ability and willingness to perform

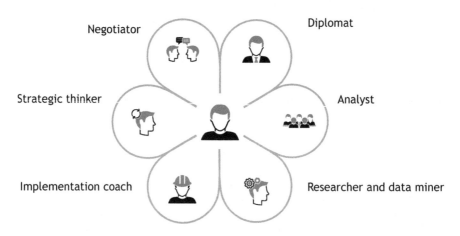

Fig. 2 Capability requirements for strategic procurement employees

are characterized by their non-redundant setup. Each day, a different skill mix is required, making it hard to plan or even robotize.

As strategic thinkers, procurement employees must define the future state of a category; for example, by setting up roadmaps while at the same time considering the available supply base. As negotiators, they conduct negotiations with both external (e.g., suppliers) and internal stakeholders (e.g., engineering), select the right negotiation approach, and prepare fact-based commercial discussions by holistically gathering information. As diplomats, they act as the core interface toward business partners and consistently challenge existing specifications. As analysts, they conduct the necessary calculations such as linear performance pricing (LPP) or simple outlier analysis. As researchers and data miners, they screen supply markets or internal data to identify and evaluate suppliers or to clean spend data prior to large tenders, for example. Finally, as implementation coaches, they ensure their savings are implemented in the organization. For this skill, procurement employees must pay close attention to detail to follow through with the required activities with a group of stakeholders, such as in engineering or plants.

By contrast, requirements made of operational procurement employees are relatively standardized. They entail, above all, a structured and detailed way of working, deep knowledge of the procure-to-pay (P2P) process and workflow in the organization, and a holistic understanding of systems to ensure efficient handling of data entries and management. As such, operational procurement employees must act as process experts in terms of being knowledgeable about systems management; as perfectionists by ensuring, for example, that prices are updated regularly; and as communicators in order to link with suppliers and track purchasing orders.

Willingness to Perform

While true that an employee's motivation is typically hard to measure, there are four dimensions that have proven to be strong contributors to it: development, rewards, and recognition, company strategy and culture, and work-life balance. Essentially, each of these dimensions focuses on creating an engaged and committed workforce. Companies developing their procurement employees, for example, might achieve this by giving them more responsibility. Rewards can be "value project of the month" awards for teams who achieved breakthrough savings, for example. A strong meritocracy culture—a system where ability and achievement are the basis for advancement—can help advance employee engagement levels and, beyond that, reduced work hours (e.g., via sabbaticals) can help sustain a healthy work-life balance.

Upcoming Challenges

Successful companies have been those that nurture the skills of their procurement employees and keep motivation high. However, although these approaches have worked well in the past, they are likely to fall short in light of the requirements of the digital revolution ahead. As such, the upcoming change requires procurement employees a more diverse skill set and it definitely requires teams to be motivated beyond previous levels—not only to go through the digital change but to shape it for their respective functions. And, most importantly, this change is coming faster than initially anticipated. In short, three upcoming challenges stand out:

- Having digital solutions take over current procurement tasks
- Ensuring development of the skills needed for new digital solutions
- Motivating buyers to drive the change needed

How Digital Is Changing the Game: Requiring Different People Profiles, Skills, and Stronger Motivation

Having Digital Solutions Take Over Current Procurement Tasks

If we look at the wide and non-redundant task set of strategic buyers, it would be difficult to replace it with purely robotic solutions. This is especially true for strategy creation or dealing with business partners (diplomat). However, other activities can at least be significantly supported by digital, making the lives of strategic buyers easier and limiting the skill set required. An example is the negotiator skill. The core task here has been to pick the right negotiation design. Now, AI can support in decision-making using negotiation coaches. These coaches significantly increase the share of auctions versus face-to-face negotiations, and robots set up the auctions automatically. Another example is the analyst skill. Big data systems can be processed using advanced analytics, such as LPPs with automated regression reports on all parts of a category shared on a monthly basis with the respective buyers. The biggest digital impact will be on the researcher and data miner role. Here, data crawlers automatically fill repositories, for instance by autonomously scanning contracts or collecting feedback from suppliers.

Based on these developments, the skill set needed from strategic buyers is changing substantially, necessitating a different people profile (see Fig. 3).

The situation looks different for operational procurement. Here, a large share of the tasks can easily be taken over by robotics. Current skills, such as the ability to structure data input and follow-ups, will be needed much less frequently. A large share of operational buyers will be freed up for more strategic tasks or for offering potential HR budget savings.

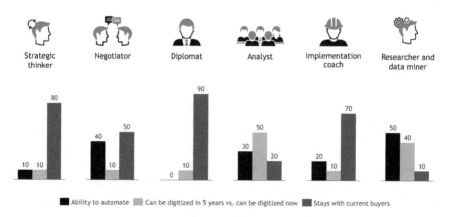

Fig. 3 Automatization of tasks for strategic buyers

Ensuring Development of the Skills Needed for New Digital Solutions

When thinking about adapting new digital capabilities in procurement, CPOs should divide their employees into three groups, each requiring a varying degree of digital adoption (see Fig. 4).

The smallest group, the *digital creators*, includes those employees at the core of digital value creation. They account for roughly 10% of the procurement function and their core competences include the creation and control of complex data models and the development of advanced algorithms. In most instances, these people have to be recruited since their skill set is new to procurement functions. Typical roles are master data specialists, AI modelers, or robotics engineers. Master data specialists, who are in charge of large data repositories, feed them with data (e.g., via data crawlers) and make sure that buyers also enter the right data points. They form the backbone of all analytics and AI. AI modelers write codes to feed advanced analytics or AI in order to support decision-making. They build AI negotiation coaches or risk management assessments that try to detect suppliers who might soon end up in financial distress. Robotics engineers design and maintain the bots that are primarily used in operational procurement. Digital change agents are also counted among the core group of digital creators, although their work does not focus on data, codes, or robotics. They ensure that digital change is accepted and embraced within the function.

The second cluster, the *digital core group*, needs to have a thorough understanding of how digital systems work. They must constantly interpret their output and, even more importantly, understand when digital solutions should be applied and what input parameters should be used. For example, a buyer for tail spend in a chemicals company first needs to realize that an AI-based solution could enable him to better predict the item portfolio in which a quality failure is likely to occur. Also, the buyer must provide the AI programmer with the relevant input parameters and

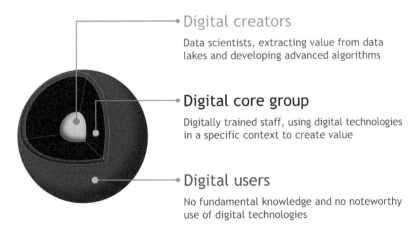

Fig. 4 Three capability types in a digitalized procurement function

then calibrate the systems to deliver the desired output. The digital core group consists of those employees who bring digital to life, expand technology to new fields, and ensure it is used to tackle day-to-day challenges. These individuals make up for another 20–30% of the function.

The third group, the *digital users*, includes those employees who usually have no fundamental understanding of the digital system. In the future, however, they will need to know how to use and interact with it. Digital users are primarily based on operational procurement and may interact with robotics in PR-PO approval, for example. Companies will need to develop the skills of digital users to interact with machines, for instance via feedback loops in supplier selections or open questions in PR approvals which the machines cannot assess themselves.

Motivating Buyers to Drive the Change Needed

The digitization of procurement goes hand in hand with an acceleration of pressure, uncertainty, and increasing requirements for value generation. Strategic purchasers will be guided in their decisions by AI and other technologies. Activities in operational procurement will largely be made redundant and the remaining operational purchasers will have to welcome robots as their new colleagues. At the same time, new specialized roles will be introduced, such as the aforementioned master data scientists or robotics engineers. While the conventional pillars of motivation will still play a large role, the change to come is too big to rely on them alone. Another paradigm has come to the fore in such turbulent times: leadership.

Thinking of procurement at the front lines of corporate value generation, it is natural to look at another organization facing similar challenges (although in a different environment) from which to draw inspiration. Jocko Willink and Leif Babin, former Navy SEALs, have coined the leadership paradigm "extreme ownership."[1] In critical missions—and this applies to digital transformation projects in procurement, too—four major principles emerge that determine success or failure: *accountability*, *discipline*, *enthusiasm*, and *communication*. With laser focus on the leadership approach in these four principles, Navy SEALs lead their teams through uncertainty and form a group ready to take on any change needed.

Accountability is probably the most important principle of extreme ownership. Accepting total responsibility, owning up to problems that inhibit performance, and developing solutions to those problems is needed to create value in digital times. Despite the uncertainty in digital times, employees need to feel fully accountable for the results they deliver. *Discipline* ensures that leaders keep sight of the strategic mission and help their team members remain flexible and adaptable to changes, such as the need to rely on AI for upcoming choices. A team can only deliver exceptional performance if they work together effectively. *Enthusiasm* ensures that procurement

---

[1]Willink, Jocko, und Leif Babin. 2015. Extreme Ownership: How U.S. Navy SEALs Lead and Win. St. Martin's Press.

leaders strive for continuous improvement and instill a similar attitude in their team members. True leadership is about making people execute difficult tasks, have them handle uncertainty, and determine the right priorities. Digital bears great opportunities, so CPOs need to spin a positive story around it. Finally, *communication* ensures that team members understand what to do and, more importantly, why they should do it. Extreme owners are true believers in their mission and always identify ways to jointly achieve that mission. They ensure that each member is part of the team and not an excuse for it.

How It Has Been Done: Procurement Transformation at a Global Bank

When a leading German bank embarked on its journey to define and implement digital transformation for its procurement function, the function's reputation in the company was rather poor. Despite the significant spend volume of €5 billion—mainly in IT—and the awareness of difficult times ahead, procurement was not considered a strategically relevant function. The CPO however, who had recently been appointed to the position and who had successfully streamlined the sales unit before, recognized the enormous potential in the function. Mainly driven by the large opportunities afforded by the digital landscape and the leverage he saw in his young team, he defined the vision of becoming the leading procurement function in the services industry. He made digital transformation the cornerstone of his agenda and communicated this clearly to both his people and other functions. But rather than simply outlining the project deliverables, he decided to take his people on a journey. Milestones were set up like a mountain climbing expedition, and each milestone was to reveal its own unique challenges. His charisma and the way he brought the digital roadmap to life created a level of enthusiasm the team had never experienced before. Each member started developing a strong sense of gratification and a continuous improvement mindset.

Another cornerstone was the savings target the CPO had initially defined: €500 million. And, going one step further still, the CPO made himself fully accountable for reaching it. He clearly communicated to the leadership team that there was only one person to blame in case of failure and that was the CPO himself. This attitude, together to become a benchmark for other functions and indeed the services industry as a whole, made every team member work harder than ever before. The procurement function was no longer made up of one leader and many followers, it was made up of many leaders working together with one representing them all.

After 15 months, the digital roadmap was successfully implemented and the savings target was even exceeded. The discipline that the CPO demonstrated throughout the transformation project was remarkable: from project kick-off on day one right through to the last day when all milestones had been implemented, he always remained focused on the strategic mission. He also

(continued)

consistently enforced high-performance standards—until they eventually became the new standard. Agile prioritization and rigorous decision-making facilitated this process.

Looking Ahead

People are *the* core pillar in any digital change. CPOs must have a good understanding of how each role in their function will be affected by the digital revolution. Equally important, they need to thoroughly understand what new roles and capabilities will be needed that have not yet been embedded in the function. The most important focus, however, will be the change management aspect of how to lead the function's employees into the new digital era in a positive yet challenging manner. The Navy SEALs' approach to leadership yields many an insight here. CPOs are well advised to adopt the principles of extreme ownership—probably the most extreme form of change management—and follow the understanding of what it takes to be successful particularly in digital times. They must be leaders and followers, straightforward but self-reflecting, diligent yet without losing perspective, and determined but always considerate. These capabilities will be crucial to claiming victory on their own unique battlefields.

Performance Management: Bridging the Value Delivered

Undoubtedly, performance management is one of the most crucial enablers for procurement success. However, few CPOs have it clearly under control. In a recent survey of approximately 50 procurement heads, only 65% stated that their performance management covered the core value dimensions driven by the function. In response to the question as to whether the performance was accurately measured, only 22% said "yes" and 9% answered in the affirmative that at least the majority of employees in the function were covered by a transparent and fair performance management system. But what keeps this core enabler scoring so low in actual implementation?

Starting Position: Performance: Measuring Value, an (Almost) Unsolvable Task

Procurement performance is defined by the value dimensions selected from the procurement house. Savings may be a dominant theme, but there is usually at least one other value dimension in focus. Only after clarifying which value dimensions really matter to the procuring company can the right KPIs be chosen. A focus on savings, for example, requires precise tracking of the cost improvements realized against previously calculated potential. Similarly, a focus on innovation requires a more abstract KPI set, such as the number of innovative suppliers identified or business partner satisfaction with procurement's innovation efforts. Overall, there are more than 200 procurement KPIs and, ultimately, each procurement function must find its own tailored set of KPIs. Fig. 1 shows an exemplary cut with two KPIs per value dimension.

Although there is a natural tendency to focus on value creation when talking about performance management, the focus on core enablers should not be underestimated: KPIs must also be defined for critical enablers and they need to be monitored with the same rigor as those focusing on value generation. Moreover, there needs to be a sound taxonomy of what constitutes the desired performance.

© Springer Nature Switzerland AG 2020
W. Schnellbächer, D. Weise, *Jumpstart to Digital Procurement*,
https://doi.org/10.1007/978-3-030-51984-1_11

DIMENSION	NAME	DEFINITION	FORMULA
SAVINGS	Recurring savings	Recurring savings are measured as a delta against the applicable baseline	*Volume delta * baseline volume* **or** *baseline volume * price delta*
SAVINGS	Project spend savings	For large, individual projects, savings are measured against the budget. For all other projects, spend is assumed to be recurring and savings are measured against the baseline	*Planned project budget − actual project budget*
INNOVATION	Innovation satisfaction	Absolute change in business partner satisfaction score with innovation work done by procurement	*Actual innovation satisfaction score − Last period satisfaction score*
INNOVATION	New supplier identification	No. of new potential suppliers identified against innovation demand defined by procurement	*No. of innovative suppliers identified against innovation demand*
QUALITY	Business partner quality satisfaction	Absolute change in business partner quality satisfaction score	*Actual quality satisfaction score − last period quality satisfaction score*
QUALITY	Parts per million	No. of defects per million items procured	$\dfrac{Defects\ due\ to\ procurement\ issues * 1{,}000{,}000}{No.\ of\ items\ procured}$
SUSTAINABILITY	Sustainability assessment coverage	% of suppliers monitored for social or environmental risk	$\dfrac{No.\ of\ suppliers\ monitored}{No.\ of\ suppliers}$
SUSTAINABILITY	Supplier sustainability rating	% of total suppliers with low CSR rating	$\dfrac{No.\ of\ suppliers\ with\ low\ CSR\ rating}{No.\ of\ suppliers}$
SPEED	PR to PO time	Average PR to PO process time (only order not solved via catalogs)	$\dfrac{\sum time\ per\ PR\ to\ PO\ process}{No.\ of\ PRs}$

Fig. 1 Example KPIs per dimension

SPEED	Vendor onboarding time	Average vendor onboarding time	$$\frac{\sum time\ required\ per\ supplier\ onboarding}{No.\ of\ suppliers\ onboarded}$$
RISK	Risk assessment coverage	% of suppliers monitored for financial and operational risk	$$\frac{No.\ of\ suppliers\ monitored}{No.\ of\ suppliers}$$
RISK	Supplier portfolio risk	% of total suppliers with high financial risk grading	$$\frac{No.\ of\ suppliers\ with\ high\ risk\ grading}{No.\ of\ suppliers}$$
ORGANIZATIONAL STRUCTURE	Spend per FTE	Spend covered per procurement FTE	$$\frac{\sum spend\ administered\ by\ procurement}{No.\ of\ procurement\ FTE}$$
ORGANIZATIONAL STRUCTURE	POs per FTE	Purchase orders handled by each procurement FTE	$$\frac{No.\ of\ PO\ handled}{No.\ of\ procurement\ FTE}$$
PEOPLE	Clear job descriptions	% of employees with clear job descriptions (including digital roles)	$$\frac{No.\ of\ employees\ with\ clear\ job\ descriptions}{No.\ of\ employees}$$
PEOPLE	Tenure with company	Average tenure of employees with the company	$$\frac{\sum employee\ years\ with\ company}{No.\ of\ employees}$$
PERFORMANCE MANAGEMENT	Performance management system	Existence of clearly defined KPIs and defined performance management system	Yes or no
PERFORMANCE MANAGEMENT	Target setting process	Existence of reasonably ambitious but achievable targets and a cross-functional target-setting process	Yes or no
COLLABORATION	Supplier satisfaction	Absolute change in supplier satisfaction with the organization's procurement function	*Actual supplier satisfaction score − last period supplier satisfaction score*
COLLABORATION	Business partner satisfaction	Absolute change in business partner satisfaction with the procurement function	*Actual business partner satisfaction score − last period business partner satisfaction score*

Fig. 1 (continued)

This task is tricky, especially in the field of savings. The challenge lies in giving equal credit to the procurement function for good performance while, at the same time, measuring the true cost-out effects for the P&L. The complexity involved between the two objectives becomes apparent when looking at the calculation of savings on items never before purchased or for raw materials that are priced against an index (e.g., steel). If, for example, the buyer purchases better relative to a rising index than in the previous year, it is considered a success. However, it is a success that is hard to explain to business partners who only see costs on the rise and who might question how the "true" performance has been in times of decreasing commodity prices. Best-in-class companies therefore run a strict internal procurement savings measurement logic that gives "true" credit to buyers based on their individual performance. As such, the function needs to strongly align all guidelines and major sign-offs with the company's CFO and the function benefitting from the savings.

In other value dimensions, complexity in measurement is similar. In innovation, for example, it is the type of innovation that the business is looking for that is decisive. If it is a previously unknown and innovative breakthrough, the number of new innovative suppliers identified might be the reference of choice. If the innovation tends more to target a less costly melting technique for frequently used metals, the fulfillment of these innovation requirements might be a feasible KPI. In any case, without input or approval from business partners, any conclusion on performance in terms of innovation, quality, or any other value dimension is likely to be either insufficient or wrong.

The difficulty of defining KPIs for value priorities also extends to the enabler dimensions. Process efficiency, for example, is complex to measure, especially if running cross-functionally and involving multiple interfaces. While the end-to-end process time is a meaningful and intuitive metric, it does not account for the accuracy of the output and thus has to be complemented by a corresponding KPI. Moreover, conclusions about the actual process efficiency and the underlying drivers can only be drawn if the run time is automatically documented for all process interfaces. Similarly, assessing employee skills and defining a training curriculum are only of limited use if they do not consider employee satisfaction with the progress they make. Last, evaluating the efforts devoted to collaboration is unlikely to yield any meaningful value without gathering input from business partners and suppliers beforehand on what constitutes good collaboration.

Overall, a clear performance taxonomy consists of three elements. First, a *baseline* for each KPI is required, one that is centrally aligned with business partners, finance, and planning. It needs to be differentiated into *price and volume baselines:*

- *Price baselines* can be based on past prices, indexes, a budget calculation (for products and services with no past buying), or a should-cost model.
- *Volume baselines* can be based on forecasts and even historic values if forecasts are not available.

Second, a *calculation methodology* for each KPI is necessary, detailing performance and how it is accounted for across a number of scenarios:

- Savings *are* considered a sustainable reduction in spending; they are differentiated by recurring and project-based effects.

- An *exception* are commodities with clear indices and high market volatility; they are evaluated against the market index to determine performance.
- *Distorting* factors such as currency or volume effects are not considered when evaluating buyer performance; these factors are not usually under a buyer's control (however, they are considered when translating procurement performance into the P&L and budget adjustments).

Third, an *approval mechanism* has to be specified, outlining how measured performance is validated and jointly approved by procurement, business partners, and finance (if applicable)—otherwise, the observed performance will be refuted and not communicated. For example, for savings,

- A *tracking* tool ensures that each savings initiative is reflected in a robust tracking sheet.
- An *approval* process ensures that savings initiatives only become valid after being signed off by finance and the business owner.

Upcoming Challenges

Even when they get all the described approaches described right, CPOs might still struggle because of two upcoming challenges:

- Ensuring that *correct* data from fragmented, inconsistent data sources is gathered into comprehensive, personalized dashboards.
- *Verifying* performance management data with reasonable effort and ensuring the right follow-ups (e.g., budget adjustments based on savings).

How Digital Is Changing the Game: A Final Verification of Procurement's Value

Ensuring that correct data from fragmented, inconsistent data sources is gathered into comprehensive personalized dashboards.

The data for performance management KPIs is available in varying maturities. While process and cycle times used to measure P2P efficiency can be drawn directly from ERP systems, the data readiness to measure savings successes largely depends on the category in focus. Data on other value and enabler dimensions often lies in completely remote systems, such as training applications that buyers use for knowledge creation or feedback they receive from suppliers. In some instances, data might not be available at all.

Big data analytics are powerful in consolidating data from landscapes that are highly fragmented and with a high consolidation need. Available solutions can pull data from various company systems or a central repository in real time, clean it using machine learning techniques, and consolidate it in a combined data lake. Following this consolidation, the data is split a second time into personalized KPI baskets to enable the presentation of the right performance views to individual FTEs. Based on these KPI baskets, each buyer is given a cockpit showing his true performance along with all relevant value and enabler dimensions. Using big data, even more complex KPIs such as time spent at process interfaces, reaction time to negative feedback, or overall PR to PO process speed can be made transparent. Leveraging these new digital opportunities enables procurement to connect personalized KPIs and dashboards with central data repositories.

Verifying performance management data with reasonable effort and ensuring the right follow-ups (e.g., *budget adjustments based on savings*).

As data increases, a greater need for data verification emerges—especially when it is consolidated from fragmented systems. Today, in times of live reporting and personalized KPIs, only few KPIs are solidly reported—and errors are often manually detected. These detections include different currencies in savings reporting (savings), distortions in process times through order outliers (speed), or simple errors such as the wrong manual data input into systems (across value and enabler dimensions). Automated verification helps tackle these distortions across a wide data portfolio and artificial intelligence plays a key role here: it detects inconsistencies and errors in performance numbers that have been generated using big data. For example, a global telecommunications provider recently installed boundaries into its performance management system with AI helping to detect implausible KPIs based on their historic development.

But AI can go even further, beyond mere performance tracking. Examples can be automated budget and P&L adjustments in response to price index or volume fluctuations. Making sure that forecasts find their way into budgets is one of the most essential exercises for materializing savings and AI can, for example, classify savings into the right cost buckets. This task used to be performed by the finance function but has become obsolete thanks to AI.

In the near future, AI will be able to (partially) manage performance autonomously, for example, by automatically informing suppliers about detected quality issues and even proposing ways of resolving them. In conclusion, the benefits of digital performance management in procurement will be derived from better and more efficient monitoring of actual performance, greater objectivity of the analysis, more precise performance forecasts due to predictive analytics, and automated management of performance through AI and pattern recognition.

How It Has Been Done: Performance Management at a Global Automobile Manufacturer

A global automobile manufacturer faced significant transparency issues with its procurement performance. Business partners questioned procurement's capabilities and claimed to be better at handling indirect procurement themselves. At the same time, the procurement function strongly believed it was

(continued)

delivering the expected performance. Moreover, the procurement function consistently reported savings significantly higher than the market average, of 4–5%. Nevertheless, business partner buy-in was limited and a feeling of unfair treatment spread among procurement staff.

To overcome the friction and create transparency on both business partner expectations and the actual performance management system, three workshops were set up with the following distinct objectives:

1. *Selection of value priorities and supporting enablers: The first workshop was held with the procurement function and followed the structure of BCG's Procurement House. During the course of an extensive discussion, the value parameters most crucial to the organization's objectives and the enablers best suited to support these objectives were identified. In terms of value objectives, securing market share in the growing e-mobility market was selected, while people, performance management, and collaboration with innovative suppliers constituted the core enablers of this proposition.*

2. *Design of KPIs: In a second internal procurement workshop, KPIs were developed for managers and buyers, reflecting the value priorities and enablers defined in the first workshop. To track collaboration with new innovative suppliers, one of the KPIs was formulated in terms of the percentage of suppliers active in innovation collaboration platforms. Equally important, KPIs were tailored to roles. Managers had KPIs dedicated to people development added to their savings or innovation-related KPIs (e.g., employee satisfaction with training and development opportunities, the percentage of employees assessed on their digital capabilities). The individual employees, in turn, were assigned not only a set of functional role-specific KPIs (e.g., savings achieved with strategic suppliers) but also development-related ones (e.g., the percentage of the training curriculum completed). Thus, every individual involved in procurement was aware of the expectations to be fulfilled.*

3. *Alignment with key stakeholders: The final workshop involved all business partners with the aim of getting their final feedback and sign-off on the value and enabler priorities as well as the KPI taxonomy and measurement logic. This part was crucial to create transparency regarding procurement's performance for business partners. Driven by a strong belief in the importance of translating savings into P&L impact, two business partners sponsored a dedicated resource for that purpose, located directly in procurement controlling. Likewise, concrete procedures for collaboration were agreed. For example, any saving exceeding €one million had to be reported directly to the relevant business partner in a special template—frequently leading to special acknowledgment of the responsible buyer.*

(continued)

Following the workshops, a performance management tool was set up and directly linked to the savings reported. The tool consisted of three major interfaces, one with the existing system landscape of the organization (i.e., the ERP, the online capability-building academy, and the collaboration platform), and the other two with procurement FTE being measured and the evaluating managers within and outside of procurement. The combination of the three interfaces allowed for automated collection of measurement-related quantitative data from company systems as well as of stakeholder input for qualitative KPIs (i.e., business partner and supplier satisfaction with procurement), ultimately allowing for automated KPI calculation and distribution of results to all roles and related parties through personalized dashboards. Overall, the review of the performance management system created unprecedented transparency on the overall strategic objectives in procurement as well as on its actual importance. The extensive involvement of the business partners proved to be essential to the process and substantially increased the credibility of the redesigned performance management system.

Looking Ahead

Performance management is a core enabler of value creation in procurement. However, only few procurement functions have it under control. CPOs should focus their performance management on the core value dimensions crucial to their business partners and equally weight the enablers supporting these. On this basis, KPIs with clear measurement logic should be installed on the selected value and enabler dimensions. In tracking these KPIs, big data needs to be heavily leveraged for collecting and cutting spend, and artificial intelligence for driving the initial conclusions in follow-ups.

Collaboration: Leveraging Business Partners in the Inside and Outside

Collaboration is defined as working with partners with the common purpose of securing benefits for the business. Faced with increasing product complexity, an expanding global supplier landscape, and the ever-rising need for alignment, managing collaboration with internal and external business partners has always been at the heart of procurement. It helps to identify internally which value dimensions (i.e., savings, innovation, quality, sustainability, speed, and risk) are most important to other functions such as R&D or production, and it helps to appropriately reflect those requirements externally when interacting with suppliers. Yet, these collaborations are often not handled optimally—without the right focus on business partners or the optimal ways of approaching them.

Proper collaboration management involves two layers. First, a *structural layer* equips procurement with the framework necessary for organizing collaboration and interaction. It serves as a skeleton and provides a solid structure for realizing core value dimensions. Second, a *relational layer*—the nerve system—is needed to facilitate exchange with business partners and to create a cooperative spirit involving mutual respect and motivation. The ability to best play out these two layers—aligned with company and procurement strategy—determines collaboration outcomes.

Starting Position: Current Best Practices in Collaborating with Business Partners

Structural Layer of Collaboration

From a structural perspective, five core elements characterize best-in-class collaboration: *Early involvement, aligned targets and incentives, operational empowerment*, and *an ongoing data exchange approach*—all tailored along with a *smart business partner clustering* (see Fig. 1). The elements apply for both internal and external collaboration.

© Springer Nature Switzerland AG 2020

W. Schnellbächer, D. Weise, *Jumpstart to Digital Procurement*,
https://doi.org/10.1007/978-3-030-51984-1_12

Fig. 1 Core structural elements for internal and external collaboration

Early involvement ensures that procurement is included as early as during the planning phase. A team involving procurement, functions (e.g., engineering, costing), and suppliers works cross-functionally on topics such as product design, manufacturing improvement, or logistics planning. For example, procurement at a global automotive OEM accompanies the end-to-end process from development to series production to safeguard supply and quality of purchase parts.

Aligned targets and incentives enable-shared goals across functions within the organization and also with suppliers. A consumer goods company for example implemented a balanced scorecard to optimize the trade-offs of business needs among different functions and business units. Best-in-class companies also excel at aligning targets with business partners outside their organization.

Operational empowerment requires a strong governance structure to mandate procurement with a challenger role along the collaboration life cycle, both internally toward other functions (e.g., on product specification) and externally toward suppliers (e.g., during performance auditing). To give an idea, procurement at a global market research company is mandated especially in direct purchasing area to sit side by side with operations on selecting suppliers for field research service and solving disputes such as on delivery quality.

The *ongoing data exchange approach* exists at every organizational level, from strategic direction setting to day-to-day operations. At a global agricultural equipment manufacturer, for example, cross-functional category councils allow senior stakeholders to jointly plan, execute, and actively steer strategic initiatives in category management.

Smart business partner clustering helps to align with partner priorities and to specifically tailor employed methods and procedures. As business partners share similarities as well as differences, clustering them appropriately enables the determination and implementation of a customized collaboration approach. Common clustering approaches toward internal partners are based on business units, geographies, or products, whereas clustering external partners typically leverages the *spend concentration/differentiation ability* matrix. This matrix guides procurement in selecting the optimal form of supplier collaboration and helps to identify those suppliers that are most suited to strategic partnerships (see Fig. 2).

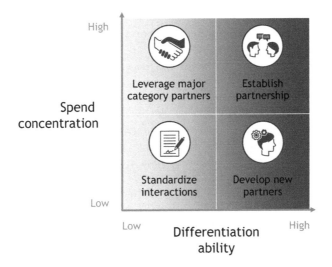

Fig. 2 *Spend concentration/differentiation ability* matrix for clustering suppliers

While *spend concentration* is assessed in terms of the ratio of category spending on a particular supplier to total category spending, *differentiation ability* with regard to perceived customer value requires more expert input; both a supplier's operational performance (e.g., cost development, quality record) and its strategic potential (e.g., product know-how, innovation capability) must be considered. The evaluation process is performed at the category level by cross-functional teams possessing both technical and commercial knowledge.

As a result, there are four different collaboration clusters. On one diagonal, the *develop new partners* cluster contains companies with limited spend but the strong potential for delivering substantial future value, while the *leverage major category partners* cluster suggests leveraging suppliers to gain operational advantages such as creating sustainable cost savings. On the other diagonal, the *standardize interactions* cluster contains a majority of suppliers that offer standardized and replaceable products or services, whereas the *established partnerships* cluster contains the smallest percentage of all suppliers. Here, the key to success is creating long-term strategic partnerships and the suppliers should be given not only the purchasing managers' but also the senior executives' full attention.

Each cluster requires a distinct method and intensity of interaction. For suppliers with *standardizing interactions,* negotiations are conducted at predefined intervals, contracts are designed uniformly, and only obligatory tasks such as audits and risk assessments are conducted by buying companies. When *establishing partnerships*, requirements for managing strategic partners are clearly defined and they involve a variety of tasks for dedicated roles within the organization. Among other things, it is important to align standards that define how to interact with suppliers, outlining for example, how often and which level of the hierarchy is involved.

> **How It Has Been Done: Supplier Collaboration at a Laser Technology and Machining Tools Company**
>
> *A global laser technology and machining tools company was under increasing pressure to reduce costs. As traditional commercial levers gradually dried up, the company decided to explore new areas of opportunity by boosting collaboration with suppliers. The company set concrete standards for managing its over 50 strategic suppliers. A dedicated supplier coordinator was nominated for each of these suppliers to ensure a single point of contact and maximum value creation. Depending on the supplier's financial impact and strategic relevance (e.g., innovation performance or the number of categories covered), either a local buyer, a category manager, or a purchasing manager was made responsible for managing the relationship. Moreover, systematic interaction was set up: supplier visits were conducted at least four times per year along with representatives from the relevant functions, such as production. Also, suppliers were granted exclusive access to the company's innovation pipeline to be able to challenge specifications early in the new product development process and thus instigate cost-saving and/or value-creating opportunities. Previously only 20% of the savings pipeline was made up of noncommercial levers (e.g., product redesign); the ratio has now risen to over 40%.*

Relational Layer of Collaboration

Besides a factual approach, interpersonal aspects are also relevant for collaborations. Elements in a clear *argumentation approach* provide a solid basis for discussions with business partners, while aspects of *influencing techniques* create the appropriate atmosphere for backing such a structure (see Fig. 3).

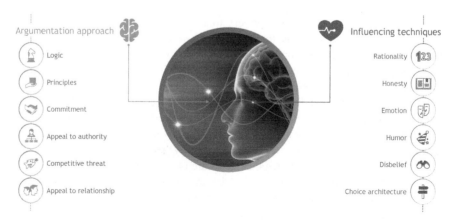

Fig. 3 Relational elements in internal and external collaboration

Argumentation approaches encompass logic, principles, commitment, appeal to authority, competitive threat, and appeal to relationship. For example, *logic* sets out a series of logical arguments justifying why a position is correct, while *principles* help to gage whether the counterpart's position is in line with the principles of, for example, the mutual relationship. Some argumentation approaches such as *logic* and *principles* can be applied to all business partners, whereas others can involve people's feelings and should be chosen with caution. For example, the *competitive threat* might work well for suppliers positioned in the *standardize interactions* cluster, but it can jeopardize collaboration with suppliers with which the company wants to *establish partnership*.

Influencing techniques include honesty, emotion, humor, disbelief, and choice architecture. Deliberate application of these techniques can, for example, help smooth the course of collaboration and maximize outcomes. For instance, being open and honest toward the counterpart helps to build trust and credibility, while a little bit of humor helps to ease the tension and can bring collaboration back on track.

How It Has Been Done: Managing Supplier Relationships at a Global FMCG Company

Years ago, a worldwide FMCG company introduced a comprehensive collaboration framework aiming to improve supplier relationships. Still, no progress was made—instead, savings realized in negotiations decreased over time. A more detailed analysis showed that traditional supplier interaction was typically stuck in a zero-sum situation, a new form of collaboration was needed. However, despite all structural elements existing, an internal survey revealed not only a poor perception of procurement's role with low value-add in collaborations but also a broken relationship between procurement and partners. The procurement team was frequently described as "rigid" and "driven by uninspired zero-sum thinking" by internal functions and suppliers. So, the company rolled out group-wide cross-functional training courses focusing on argumentation and influencing techniques. In the trainings, participants from procurement were grouped with for example R&D or production colleagues to jointly solve business challenges. In supplementary coaching sessions, communication experts instructed buyers during simulated negotiations on how to best apply relational elements in internal and external collaborations.

The training took effect. 2 years later, not only a self-assessment showed greatly improved confidence in and perception of collaboration capabilities, the company was also highly recognized in the industry for its strict but fair management of supplier relationships. For those suppliers that successfully achieved the targets, the company showed its commitment toward the relationship by sharing the achieved outcomes, for example, cost reductions. Still, the company continued to regularly conduct an extensive performance

---

(continued)

assessment and peer benchmarking of suppliers; results and especially performance gaps were clearly laid out. The company also made it clear to suppliers that they would be phased out if the gaps could not be justified or closed in time. By always acting faithfully toward its suppliers, the company has proved its credibility, which has resulted in deep collaborations, for example, with suppliers willing to open their books. These approaches and techniques helped the company to establish a win-win relationship on a long-term basis.

Upcoming Challenges

Successful procurement organizations across industries are able to align targets with internal functions and identify the right suppliers for creating strong partnerships. However, while these approaches have worked well in the past, they are likely to fall short when it comes to seizing the immense opportunities offered by the looming digital revolution.

CPOs must critically think through how to steer the changes that digitization brings to their collaborations. The upcoming changes require procurement to be able to leverage the digital tools and approaches available. In particular, two challenges stand out:

– Connecting widespread information sources to develop collaborative wisdom.
– Leveraging AI defined service and product clusters to tailor collaboration approaches.

How Digital Is Changing the Game: Tackling the Barriers of Collaboration

Connecting Widespread Information Sources to Develop Collaborative Wisdom

In a traditional approach, an innovation inquirer either reaches out to the academic world, industry association, or suppliers already known. Technical workshops are organized in physical form or per video conference, which is both time consuming and inefficient.

Avant-garde companies start exploiting new digital opportunities to better connect widespread information sources with stakeholders in the whole ecosystem and to collaboratively work on business needs. The digital innovation platforms, for example, provide a virtual collaboration space that can be accessed anytime by both internal and external business partners. The posted requests for creative solutions are seen and answered immediately by a variety of players including existing suppliers, unknown start-ups, academic scholars, or even "hidden" innovation champions within the same company from other locations. This open environment significantly extends the border of the ecosystem and minimizes white spots in innovation identification. A multinational consumer appliance and technology corporation, for example, implemented an open innovation platform where internal stakeholders and suppliers can work together on solutions to meet company's needs. A leading life sciences company opened an online platform to enable agile exchange with suppliers on business challenges and possible solutions. Especially smaller non-incumbent suppliers used this opportunity to connect to the life science company and show their innovation potential.

Other companies utilize technology scouting enabled by big data to detect recent innovations or identify emerging trends within the sector. Such technology engines leverage automated data analytics and machine intelligence to extract and process data around preset topics from diverse databases and expert networks. The results are structured and presented in a visualized form to highlight, e.g., technology break-through or tipping points of trends. For instance, a European diary company embedded a trend detection technology into its management process to enable early spotting of inspirations for new business opportunities.

Leveraging AI Defined Service and Product Clusters to Tailor Collaboration Approaches

Most companies today fall short of unlocking their suppliers' full capabilities to address challenges, not to mention being able to identify new suppliers in order to harvest upcoming opportunities. In the future, AI-enabled technology can support buying companies to harness external innovation capabilities more effectively in order to develop increased value-add for customers. It assists internal functions in forming a fitting and focused strategy and based on this, find the best-suited suppliers, award according to the envisioned collaboration strategy and execute according to a predefined collaboration clustering.

As starting point, AI can support the definition of an innovation sourcing strategy, such as splitting complex service requirements or product developments into separate modules (e.g., defining the best split between MRO[1] components to foster supplier bundling) or identifying the optimal integration of components into a package (e.g., partitioning software with hardware elements in autonomous driving technology to optimize interface management). With such clusters, potential barriers like company size or one-stop-shop offerings are lowered and more suppliers, including startups, are both able and incentivized to participate in, e.g., RfPs, so that the maximum external knowledge can be leveraged. AI can also make recommendations on potential suppliers likely to deliver the best outcome, giving

---

[1]Maintenance, repair, and operations

internal functions the task of assessing those recommendations and then taking action toward implementation.

Depending on the strategy chosen in the earlier defined cluster, a tailored collaboration approach is proposed and implemented. The digital platform can be configured accordingly so that all interactions, such as ongoing editing and the submission of concepts as well as feedback can be performed directly on the platform, simplifying collaborative work among multiple partners. Functions owning business demand sit side by side with procurement in a joint evaluation committee to ensure that suppliers with maximum innovation power and business suitability are transparently selected.

How It Has Been Done: AI-Supported Innovation Scouting at a Leading Premium Auto Manufacturer

Under changing market conditions, traditional procurement approaches like global sourcing or forward sourcing are becoming less effective at identifying the best-suited suppliers. A leading premium auto OEM turned to AI for help. It partnered with a startup to leverage its capabilities in digital scouting enabled by an AI-driven suite. For each scouting request, either aiming for savings or innovation, the case was specified by the OEM and enriched—with help of AI recommendations—with all the relevant keywords for crucial components, for example, "LIDAR sensor." The specification and these keywords formed the criteria setting for scouting. The AI algorithm started by leveraging the spend concentration/differentiation ability matrix to quickly execute a focused effort on existing suppliers, assessing their suitability in regards to the scouting request. As the next step, all available media were screened to identify potential new suppliers that match defined specifications and keywords. Furthermore, the subsequent supplier communication and sourcing process were performed directly via a dedicated platform. After awarding, suppliers were integrated and (re-)clustered in the spend concentration/differentiation ability matrix to directly derive a tailored interaction process, consistent with the company's overall collaboration approach. Doing so allows us to further simplify collaborative work in the future, e.g., by customized questions during an RfP process.

The effect of applying such an intelligent and streamlined process was enormous. Finding suppliers for innovative finished products, for example, used to take 1–2 years, but now takes only some months depending on complexity. Furthermore, the associated internal costs were significantly reduced (in selected cases by up to 80%).

Looking Ahead

As a traditional point of contact between internal functions and external suppliers, procurement offers the potential of integrating all information sources to generate maximal value from collaboration. This potential has to be unlocked by exploiting the possibilities opened up by digitization and technology development. Completely mobilizing the extended ecosystem and fully leveraging suppliers represent the focus of collaboration in the digital age. To address these challenges, CPOs need to make timely decisions and bold moves. We believe that companies that make the right investments will seize opportunities and gain an advantage over competitors in the future.

Part III

Digital Foundation: The Basis of All Our Decisions

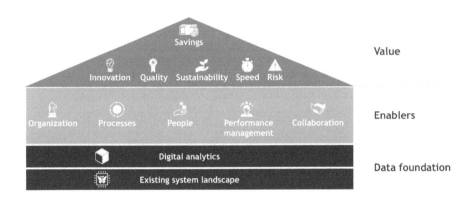

Digital Analytics: The Data Foundation for the Next Procurement Revolution

The previous chapters have shown how drastically digital will change both the work and impact of procurement. This change will particularly affect the way in which decisions are made—much less dependent on intuition and more on big data leveraged for AI-based algorithms. As digital analytics detects patterns in existing data and predict future developments, it helps buyers to make smarter, better-informed business decisions than ever before. Big data also builds the foundation for AI and blockchain, facilitates collaboration between business partners, and ensures that robotics makes the right decisions. Understanding data and performing the right analyses thus serves as the backbone of digitization.

But what do we as procurement professionals need to do to ensure this treasure trove is appropriately leveraged to make the right decisions? What repetitive steps are necessary for gathering and analyzing data correctly? What do we need to do to ensure that it is built correctly and is always up to date? The following subchapters provide a thorough overview of the way digital analytics works.

Four Steps to Unleash the Full Value Potential

Given that the data structures and strategic foci of businesses differ, every digital analytics model must be tailored to a company's peculiarities. Therefore, to unleash the full value potential of digital in procurement, buyers must follow four steps.

1. *Gather relevant data and create a holistic database:* First, it is essential to gather the existing data. To allow for more precise analyses, external data sources such as supplier financials or traffic data are often included. Next, the data is pooled in one single format and prepared for further processing by correcting format errors or excluding outliers (e.g., outdated purchase orders). Finally, all scattered data is integrated into a structured, holistic data lake for further development.
2. *Visualize data to fine-tune the scope:* The next step is to generate hypotheses based on an initial visualization of the data. By using stochastic techniques such

© Springer Nature Switzerland AG 2020   111
W. Schnellbächer, D. Weise, *Jumpstart to Digital Procurement*,
https://doi.org/10.1007/978-3-030-51984-1_13

as correlations and clustering, data scientists can prioritize variables and determine which should ultimately be integrated into the data model (e.g., if meteorological effects systematically influence timeliness in logistics). Clear hypotheses help to refine the problem set that ultimately lays the foundation for constructing the analytical model. The key outcome of this step is alignment on the questions that need to be answered by the analytical model.

3. *Build the digital analytics model:* Having defined the questions to be answered, the digital analytics model can be developed (usually by data scientists). The model construction cycle is initiated by selecting the model that best fits the data and desired outcome, such as the demand forecast for a certain commodity. This is followed by the process of model training, where relationships are coded in order to "train" the model. In this process, the model learns, for example, how expected demand for the end product translates to requisite purchase orders for parts of a commodity. The final step in the cycle is model evaluation, which helps to revise the model's performance. The model is then iterated by running through the cycle until the desired model quality is reached. Last, the desired output format for meeting user requirements is selected.

4. *Automate and customize the model:* Once the data modeling has been completed, the algorithms to be used are automated. Moreover, a fixed database connection is established and a user interface for day-to-day use developed. With a convenient interface, commodity buyers can, for example, immediately create an overview of how a changed demand forecast for the end product translates to volume changes for parts in their commodities. This interface can then display a ranking of the most effective tender approaches or illustrate a selection of suppliers for certain part purchases based on the changed demand forecast, supplier financials, geopolitical risk data, and other variables.

How It Has Been Done: Digitization of Decision-Making at a Large Food Producer

A global food producer intended to optimize its procurement process and reduce spend. The company had an excellent track record in the commercial aspects of procurement but had no substantial understanding of IT to enhance the impact of traditional procurement levers (e.g., by applying advanced analytics to consolidate fragmented spend that comprised over 400 ingredients and 1800 packaging types). Therefore, the company brought in external data scientists to work with the procurement function on creating a holistic database.

The team jointly prioritized relevant data based on initial hypotheses, discussing generated insights with posters in a "war room." In this process, first insights into savings potential were identified, for example, in price-elasticity analyses (see Fig. 1). *Based on the insights generated,*

(continued)

approximately 100 analyses with relevant variables were refined and the scope for further modeling detailed.

Based on the prioritized variables, data scientists initiated the modeling process cycle. They back tested the model by comparing historical results with predicted results for the same period until the desired accuracy was achieved.

The analytics model had meanwhile been successfully integrated into the procurement function and had reduced spending by 8%. Furthermore, the supplier default risk had decreased, as potential supplier quality issues were much more transparent.

Ensuring Long-Lasting Change through Digital

Businesses looking to revolutionize their procurement function need to consider implementing certain fundamental changes. Five major factors are particularly relevant:

1. *Create a digital analytics group:* As already discussed in the chapter on organization, an advanced analytics team must be established for digital analytics to reveal its potential in procurement. This dedicated group of data experts creates a holistic data view, connects data sources, and extracts value from data lakes.
2. *Ensure data rigidity in processes:* New processes are essential for promoting speed and for the cost-efficient handling of data and its models. Clear process

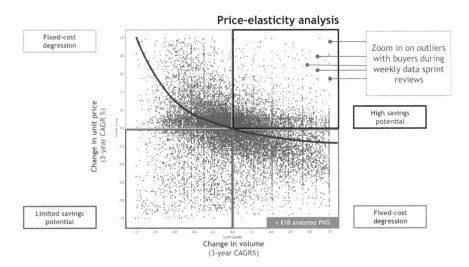

Fig. 1 Volume versus price increase: classical procurement analysis to identify outliers that indicate savings potential

descriptions must be defined for new procurement data collection, the related quality requirements, and integration thereof into the analytics model.

3. *Define a clear digital capability landscape:* In order to effectively use data models in the current system landscape, businesses should focus on a specific team composition. In the organization chapter, we learned about new roles; in the people chapter, we learned what skill sets are needed. To enable analytics, it is especially the role of master data managers and specialists for AI-based steering that must be strengthened. In addition, it needs to be ensured that strategic buyers have the relevant skill set to detect where exactly in their challenges analytics will lead to a breakthrough and which data points are needed to draw the right conclusions. The master data team can dig out relevant data and AI experts can help with the programming; however, both will have to be guided by the category buyers who have the deepest expertise in their specific challenges.

4. *Create an agile IT infrastructure:* To guarantee high-quality data input, procurement functions must ensure comprehensive data gathering with subsequent data handling. In doing so, it will be necessary to extract data from different functions and sources and to consolidate the data into one procurement database. As a final step, the output calculated and data extracted must be included in an IT solution that fits into the existing procurement tool landscape.

Overall, even though it is possible to harness considerable value with smart bolt-on niche applications, a more fundamental system integration and upgrade will become necessary as companies progress in their digital procurement ambitions.

Establish Governance to Monitor the Change Process

A governance body should be set up to monitor the changes mentioned and identify the need for action early on. Furthermore, performance indicators should be implemented so that procurement employees can better monitor individual performance and customize training courses based on specific needs. These can include, for example, percentages of decisions made that are based on digital analytics recommendations.

How It Has Been Done: A Successful Transformation Story
A Europe-wide oil and gas company introduced advanced analytics. The main goals were to improve quality and prevent risks. To improve quality, a dedicated program focusing on instantaneous data availability was initiated. Users at the sites were enabled to provide direct feedback on supplier quality by means of an application installed on their smartphones. Suppliers regularly received a transparent evaluation of user feedback and were incentivized to improve quality in relation to a jointly defined baseline. Eventually, overall

(continued)

quality performance improved by 38%, as measured by a lower PPM. In terms of risk prevention, three dimensions were identified that were responsible for bad quality and non-delivery by suppliers:

1. *Financial pressure/distress of the supplier.*
2. *Disruptions in the supply chain.*
3. *Delivery shortages caused by suboptimal, vertical organization of the supplier.*

By applying advanced analytics to a comprehensive dataset, it was possible to cluster and detail the main risk drivers in these dimensions. Ongoing analyses identified high-risk suppliers, so that only c-parts were sourced from them. As a result, a regular internal survey revealed that the perceived risk exposure to suppliers had decreased by 16%.

To achieve these results, the company needed to transform its procurement function, starting by establishing a direct report to the CPO for Research & Analytics. As a next step, processes for procurement data handling were defined. Included in the new performance management process was the way employees passed on data to the Research & Analytics group, backed by an individual performance-based bonus for clean data handling. In terms of capability types, new profiles were defined especially for the Research & Analytics unit to manage procurement data, specialize in the application of analyses, and develop advanced digital analytics tools. Implementing these fundamental changes ensured lasting improvements along the value dimensions in scope.

How to Navigate the Jungle of Possibilities to Unleash the Full Value Potential

We believe that procurement functions that successfully implement digital analytics within their existing system landscape must follow a "think big, start small, grow fast" mindset. The foundation can be laid by integrating digital analytics into the existing system landscape. However, the entire procurement function will have to be adapted to ensure it stays on track in this new digital age. Overall, decision-makers have to seize the opportunity to unlock the potential hidden in their existing data and leverage it to propel their entire business toward a sustainable future in the digital age.

Finally, a Look at the Technology

We have seen the power of digital and how it can help tackle some of procurement's core pain points across value and enabler dimensions. We have seen machines becoming smarter than us when it comes to knowing how best to negotiate to achieve great savings, advising us as to which suppliers are more innovative. We have seen that machines are faster than we are in almost any procurement process, and we have seen machines enabling collaboration much more efficiently than humans ever could.

But what are the underlying patterns? Is it always a new and unique technology, or are there recurring structures that help us better understand the functionality of digital? Considering the endless range of systems, tools, and applications out there, there are essentially five different types of solution that have been applied. Knowing these five makes it easier to grasp the breadth of the different market offerings and to create a more useful structure to help avoid potential pitfalls or application difficulties inherent in the individual solution types.

RPA/Bots

These are the human's little helpers that take care of redundant and repetitive tasks. A bot is a program trained to complete a specific task just as a human would be trained for single working steps. Its portfolio of activities includes turning purchasing requests into purchase orders by checking their validity and automatically filling out PO forms, transferring data from the PR, and extracting additional data points from different company systems. In the field of digital procurement applications, RPA represents an almost commoditized technology with many players in the market who have automated traditional processes such as PR-PO numerous times and even leveraged best-cost-country programming. The challenges in RPA for procurement, therefore, lie less in the technological rollout or the costs. The key difficulty is a natural resistance to this technology, particularly in operational procurement teams. While AI or big data are seen to help bring new insights to

© Springer Nature Switzerland AG 2020   117
W. Schnellbächer, D. Weise, *Jumpstart to Digital Procurement*,
https://doi.org/10.1007/978-3-030-51984-1_14

strategic activities, implementing bots triggers the fear of headcount reductions. CPOs need to ensure that the benefits of the technology are visible and the fear dispelled that automation simply enables headcount reduction. Companies that have been successful in communicating this typically build the storyline that their employees are too valuable for the repetitive "mundane" tasks and need to be freed up to concentrate on more strategic activities. Next to the task of managing staff resistance to RPA, there is the challenge of integrating RPA smoothly into human activities that control and intersect with processes led by bots. In addition, RPA needs to be connected well to other technologies, especially to artificial intelligence. AI can make bots much more powerful by expanding process automation beyond steps in which a particular decision needs to be taken. In PR-PO automation, for example, RPA would need the full information overview including a category code to choose the right purchasing channel and proceed. PRs that miss that information cannot be driven forward and human interference would be needed. AI, on the other hand, can be trained to deduce the right category code based on other information points, such as the category description or the supplier sample, and through that enhance RPA solutions.

> **How It Has Been Done: RPA at a Construction Materials Manufacturer**
> *A construction materials manufacturer used RPA to compare purchase orders (POs) and invoices to determine whether suppliers were charging more for their products than the prices listed on the POs. This process uncovered some substantial overcharges and the company used the information to recover 2% of total spending.*

Big Data and Advanced Analytics

These can be thought of as "our memory on steroids." In the past, information—especially of a technical and less of a commercial nature—was fragmented across company systems. Big data easily creates comprehensive overviews of that data. It enables the detection of supplier overpricing, the right performance incentivization of buyers based on more granular and timely KPI overviews or transparent quality feedbacks, and reports to suppliers by gathering information from numerous sites. Big data and analytics are a rather mature technology and oftentimes offered by big digital players that also own parts of the ERP systems. A core challenge in big data applications is embedding big data requirements into company processes. While RPA-based data crawlers can gather a lot of information from various systems, the information needs to be stored first. Often technical data points, in particular, are not properly maintained, for instance when a supplied part is changed relative to the original drawing. Big data will then arrive at the wrong conclusions, leading to lost value and buyer frustration. The proper feeding into master data systems needs to become a core performance dimension for buyers and also other procurement stakeholders—both internally and on the supplier side.

How It Has Been Done: Big Data at an Automotive Manufacturer

An automotive manufacturer needed a better understanding of the costs of the machined parts it purchased from suppliers. The company collected data from 15 million production orders in ERP across 20 global sites, specification data for more than one million parts from the PLM product data management system, and invoice prices from more than 250,000 invoice records from the FICO credit score system. Analysis of changes in unit prices and volumes over the previous 3 years made it possible to discover any supplier failure to provide the appropriate volume discounts. With this information, the company was able to renegotiate with some suppliers and, in some cases, find new ones. Consequently, the manufacturer realized associated material cost savings of 5–10% on the relevant spending volumes.

AI

AI comes closest to replicating our decision and thought processes in procurement. It leverages every information point it can get and tries to reach conclusions based on it to make the right choices. AI improves the choices that buyers today mostly have to make based on their own intuition. The advanced algorithms behind AI make it possible to quickly identify the best solution during complex negotiations involving a number of different suppliers or scenarios, for example. AI is also useful for collecting supply market intelligence, automating distinctive cognitive parts of the tender process, and improving demand forecasting. Compared to RPA or big data, AI is by far less widespread in procurement functions today and is considerably less mature. CPOs need to be more patient with this technology and allow for more trial and error. If AI is leveraged right, it can lead to the highest benefits of all digital procurement technologies since it guides buyers at the heart of their value generation—their strategic decisions.

How It Has Been Done: AI at a Consumer Packaged Goods (CPG) Company

Typical AI case: A CPG company faced the challenge of its buyers insufficiently leveraging best-in-class procurement tools. They often used face-to-face negotiations instead of auctions, war-game negotiation preparations, or supplier days. An AI negotiation coach was instituted that guided buyers to choose the right tool in every case. The usage of advanced tools increased by

---

(continued)

> *more than 40%. Even more importantly, the right tool was used in the right situation and in the right design, attuned to different auction setups. The company's savings went up by 3% during that time.*

Collaboration

Humans interact well in any face-to-face and personal setting. Collaboration software brings teams closer together, ensures timely information sharing, and facilitates discussions across time and location zones. These solutions are typically built as platforms and are used to facilitate cross-team discussions involving procurement, suppliers, and internal stakeholders such as engineering, R&D, or production functions. They may tackle issues such as cross-functional idea generation for technical savings levers, innovation ideas, or discussions on how to overcome quality issues. Collaboration solutions are quite well-known in the market, but they undergo constant improvements and changes that make them more interactive and increase the "human touch" in Internet-based interaction. A common pitfall in the implementation of collaboration solutions is relying too much on the technology itself. As powerful as its features may be, it is crucial to invite the right partners to the platform and give tailored incentives for their collaboration.

How It Has Been Done: Collaboration at a Machining Producer
A large machining producer wanted to provide its suppliers with better guidance in quality control. Using a collaboration platform, they directly shared with suppliers the quality feedback on different products and services from their sites. In addition, a procedure matched the delivered products with the respective supplier plant. In addition to that information, there were virtual problem-solving boards on which all core stakeholders could submit ideas to counter negative quality developments in specific locations.

Blockchain

As this verification technology ensures authenticity of products or information across multiple transactional steps, blockchain is the human's crystal ball, telling us whether or not the information we receive is actually true. Blockchain is known primarily for its ability to authenticate financial transactions, but this emerging technology can also be used to verify product legitimacy and origins, eliminating the costs of inspection and certification. Of all the technologies introduced, blockchain is certainly the one that has been least used in procurement to date.

When implementing blockchain, CPOs need to ensure they find the right partners for implementation in a market with little implementation know-how in procurement.

How It Has Been Done: Blockchain at a Diamond Producer

A large diamond producer faced the challenge of a continuous risk of carrying blood diamonds in their offering, since it was hard to establish full transparency along the entire supply chain. Based on a unique blockchain code for each diamond, the company was able, for the first time ever, to verify the authenticity of its diamonds from the mine to stores around the globe. Not only did it markedly reduce the risk of the company being blamed for unethical behavior, it has been perceived as a technological breakthrough in the industry.

Utopia Versus Dystopia: A Brief Look at the Decades Ahead

Analysis of digital procurement reveals many exciting, even mind-blowing developments. Not only for the value we generate as buyers, but also and even more so for how we work and the ability to train our focus on what truly matters.

RPA and smarter system integrations take over the mundane tasks such as PR checks, PO creation, or invoice checking. Big data helps us to identify more patterns, connections, and insights. AI becomes the coach that guides us with the cumulative knowledge drawn from a wide portfolio of experience, collaboration brings us closer together, and blockchain provides us with proof of the truth of sources. We are relieved of tedious tasks and help is provided for tackling the more interesting ones.

Yet as exciting as all of these developments are, they equally bear the potential to scare us. Procurement functions will have to significantly change their setup, day-to-day working procedures, and, perhaps most radically, they will have to assess who they employ. A large share of the operational headcount will no longer be needed. Among the strategic buyers, too, many may not be able to cope sufficiently with the new technologies: for example, when being guided by an AI tool on how to deal with suppliers. A dark scenario describes the future, especially if we look more than 5 years into the ahead when digital technologies will have fully unfolded in the procurement world.

This dark scenario is shaped by three main pillars. A reduced human contribution, a sole focus on efficiency, and nothing to really attract top talent to procurement. As we have seen, robotics have already taken over many of the operational, repetitive tasks and this trend will continue as systems get integrated better and better and even robotics no more will be needed. AI can make better decisions on the basis of datasets than buyers can be based on their intuition alone. We are seeing evidence of this when it comes to choosing the right negotiation strategy or the most innovative supplier. If we think ahead to a time when all companies will be able to more powerfully store their master data and make use of it in smart algorithms, the range of machine-driven choices will expand significantly. But if it is machines that are calling the shots and making the decisions, will the remaining tasks not be purely executional in those cases where some human interaction is needed, as in the case of

© Springer Nature Switzerland AG 2020   123
W. Schnellbächer, D. Weise, *Jumpstart to Digital Procurement*,
https://doi.org/10.1007/978-3-030-51984-1_15

supplier discussions, for example, What tasks will remain that require the human intellect? If all core choices are made by AI, such as regarding optimal auction design, if robotics then sets up the auction autonomously and even sends out the supplier invitations and communication, buyers will have no other choice but to sit back and watch what happens. It may sound exciting at first, but that will soon change. Moreover, if the human contribution is reduced so drastically that the core differentiating factor for CPOs in their people management is a complete focus on efficiency with the leanest function having as few buyers as possible, given their limited added value, who will be relevant in procurement? What type of talent will be attracted to these internal, efficiency-focused functions with low added value? A dystopian function with undiscernible value creation, a commoditized task portfolio, and a focus on efficiency driven by not-so-talented people.

However, there is a brighter alternative. If we as procurement professionals leverage digital right, we can greatly expand our contribution to our companies' value generation. We can still turn out to be THE winners of the upcoming digital change. At present, most stakeholders see us only as a driver of savings, a role in which we have been strong since General Motors instituted global sourcing in the late 1980s. Digital can indeed not only significantly enhance that monetary value contribution through analytics or AI-based steering, it can ensure that we also deliver on enhancing innovation, quality, sustainability compliance, or delivery speed, while significantly limiting our companies' risk exposure. This book has shown many powerful examples. In the past, we sat as though paralyzed in front of an endless parts portfolio, having no clue as to where the next quality failure might occur. Today, AI gives us clear hints up front that we can act on. In the past, we struggled with limited staff and many compliance requirements slowing our processes. Now, robotics accelerates procurement speed substantially. In terms of innovation, collaboration platforms connect us closely to core suppliers and, in risk prevention, AI is able to tell us which is the most powerful lever. In the coming years, our function will significantly increase in its positioning.

As an initial step, we need to do a thorough assessment of the status quo in conventional and digital approaches and a serious review of both what the company truly expects from its procurement and of which value dimension is most crucial for the company. Based on this, it is possible to derive the roadmap for tackling more essential challenges and recognize the enabler dimensions most required. To facilitate focused development and maximize the value of return on investment, centralizing resources around the most essential enablers is the key. Fig. 1 outlines a *value/enabler matrix* to help procurement. This matrix illustrates the level of relevance of the respective enabler to each value dimension and key points of development to boost the value proposition. Enablers ranked as "slightly relevant" must not be completely ignored. The most relevant enablers, however, should be given maximum attention and secure the commitment of management for procurement transformation in the digital era.

CEOs who take procurement seriously and enable it digitally will have significant advantages over their competitors—regardless of the industry. But what about us as procurement professionals? Will we become the slaves of machines that tell us what

	Organization	Processes	People	Performance Mgt.	Collaboration
SAVINGS	★★★ ☆ ☆ · Centering on categories with high potential · Role profile adapting	★★★ ☆ ☆ · Early involvement · Procurement mandate	★★★★★ · Commercial plus technical skill set · Motivation to challenge · Cost-consciousness	★★★★★ · Incentivization · Clear/rigid guidelines · True savings reporting · P&L linkage	★★★ ☆ ☆ · Collaboration mechanism/guideline
INNOVATION	★★★ ☆ ☆ · Focused resource assignment	★★★★★ · Early involvement · Inclusion and proper treatment of innovative suppliers	★★★ ☆ ☆ · Tailored skill set (incremental vs. breakthrough)	★★★ ☆ ☆ · Incentivization · Tailored KPI set (incremental vs. breakthrough)	★★★★★ · Clear guidelines on joint working · Trust & relationship · Closer and more frequent exchange
QUALITY	★★ ☆ ☆ ☆	★★★★★ · Embedding quality into strategy and processes · Running of technical quality tests	★★★★★ · Digitally skilled, cross-functional team · Predicting/preventing instead of fixing issues · Training programs	★★★★ ☆ · Inclusion quality into assessment · Unified quality goals	★★★★ ☆ · Onboarding/training all business partners · Clear supplier communication
SUSTAIN-ABILITY	★★★★ ☆ · Role profile adapting	★★★★★ · Embedding sustainability into strategy and processes · Regular sustainability assessment · Balancing of value dimensions in target	★★★★ ☆ · Change of mindset · Training and guidance on sustainability in procurement · Up-to-date knowledge	★★★★ ☆ · Inclusion sustainability into assessment · Reporting both threats and success stories	★★★★★ · Clear communication to business partners · Common understanding and commitment · Joint transparency on sustainable supply chain
SPEED	★★ ☆ ☆ ☆	★★★★★ · Lean processes · Clear process definition · Common understanding	★★★★★ · Up-to-date knowledge · Training programs · Team buy-in of optimized processes	★★★★★ · Process speed tracking and reporting · Process compliance monitoring	★★ ☆ ☆ ☆
RISK	★★★★ ☆ · Role profile adapting	★★★★ ☆ · Embedding risk into end-to-end processes · Regular risk assessment	★★★★★ · Risk awareness · Training and guidance on risk management · Leveraging digital tools	★★★★★ · Inclusion risk into assessment · Preventive vs. reactive · Incentivization	★★★★ ☆ · Joint transparency on supply chain risk

Legend: Level of relevance ★☆☆☆☆ Not relevant ★★★☆☆ Moderately relevant ★★★★★ Very relevant

Fig. 1 Value/enabler matrix for orientation

do, allowing us little room for creativity? How can we compete, in terms of the value we generate with our decisions, with AI-based algorithms that leverage masses of data? To answer this question, we need to keep in mind that "submarines don't swim," in other words, any technology is only as strong as the people who have built it and are using it. Yes, AI can make the best choices on how to negotiate. But buyers first have to set up the system, modify it where necessary over time, select the right data points to be fed into it, and ensure that robots feed it into the tools, such as the AI negotiation coach. Following the recommendation produced by such tools as the AI negotiation coach, the buyer might have to alter the machine-based decision, particularly when the specific context does not allow for the AI coach's choice to be implemented. And, last but not least, if the coach does not recommend an auction or any other automated bidding procedure, buyers still have to negotiate themselves. The same is true for finding innovative suppliers. AI can indicate which supplier offers the highest potential, but buyers will have to weigh up that choice within the context of their personal supplier relationship—something that a machine will never be able to do properly. Even more importantly, the buyer will have to make the case to the supplier and motivate him to enter into innovation collaboration in a personal conversation. Digital can help us, especially when it comes to taking care of redundant tasks, and it can guide and coach us based on its large data processing capabilities. In the end, however, all machines need to be set up and fed content with the expertise that only buyers have. All core strategic choices will have to be made by humans, heavily leveraging AI-based advice.

What remains is the exact opposite of a dystopia: The utopia of a function with significantly increased value added and a complex task portfolio with high techno-logical leverage, making it attractive to top talent. We strongly believe that this second, positive scenario is indeed possible if we as procurement professionals are getting it right; if we take on the challenge of a digitized world; if we do not give way to fear, but confidently move forward to make it happen.